Preface and Acknowledgements

Currently I am a Supervisor of Correctional Education Programs at the California Department of Corrections and Rehabilitation, in charge of statewide face to face college programs.

I spent 25 years in active practice as a trial lawyer, and financial attorney. As a thank you to the military who invigorated my educational career, I will annually donate, so long as I am alive, 50% of my share as author of the net profits of this book to a military charity of my choice, which may include the VFW, Disabled American Veterans, etc. I do this because as Americans we should always remember that we owe everything we see, and I mean literally everything, to our men and women in uniform.

The book is entitled Guerrilla Speech Tactics because it deals with low tech but effective methods to improve your speech or presentation. If you want focused group tested, or as Bill Clinton would say "kid tested and mother approved" sound bites, you need to hire Dick Morris. Even if you are going to use focus groups, this book will provide sound basics so that you can best use what you get from that investment.

To enhance the learning experience you should also use the internet and look at several of the best speakers available on tape. Colin Powell's briefing to the UN on why we should invade Iraq, Ross Perot's presentations during his presidential campaign, any of Rev. Billy Graham's sermons, all provide stellar examples that the reader can use to see the kinds of techniques I speak about in action. This will make the learning experience as hi tech as I can get it for the reader.

As to acknowledgments, I want to thank my wife Mary and children Michael and Elise for all of their support during the years I gained the experience in the school of hard knocks on which these lessons are based. I also want to thank Mr. Rick Moniz, Col. Brad Jones, SGM Mike Mendoza, SGM Alex Cabassa, First Sgt Carlos Arguinzoni-Gil, SGT Saul Alvarado, MSGT Carl Weston, MSGT James Patton, SGT Norris Cowles, for all their support during my two tours at OMI and Mrs Cecilia Mendoza, Mrs. Yolanda Carrillo, for their support thereafter. A special thanks to Ms. Julia A. Schappals, who urged me to write books back in 1978.

I also want to thank my late parents [while alive they said they would push up some extra daisy's if I wrote a book] SSGT Adolfo R. Ramirez, [U.S.Army 1941-45, 29th Inf Div. 116th RCT, 121st Combat Eng. Bn. Co B] a D-Day veteran, and Angela Ramirez and my in laws Jose B. and Arlene and Jose A. Mayo, for their constant support; and my former students, from whom I learned a great deal.

David M. Ramirez,
Placerville, California

GUERRILLA SPEECH TACTICS

Chapter 1 . GETTING RID OF THE JITTERS

No less a public speaker than Winston Churchill observed, "The hardest thing in the world to do is deliver an after dinner speech." Helicopter Pilot Chief Warrant Officer Ron Young, on his return from being an Iraqi POW said as he faced the entire nation over TV. and radio, along with an assemblage of hundreds of soldiers at Fort Hood, "This makes you almost as nervous as being shot at." Jerry Seinfeld once said about speaking that "when you go to a funeral more people would rather be in the box than delivering the eulogy." All of these observations truly sum up what most people think about public speaking, it is one of our great fears. This book is a guide for those who do not have expensive speech coaches, about to how to teach yourself to be an effective public speaker. It is a distillation of the lessons the author has learned from public speaking disasters and successes. It is also a culmination of study of speech and debate and the art of marketing that has spanned more than a quarter of a century. This book contains specific do's and don'ts, all of which have been tested in the school of hard knocks, both by myself and those gleaned from history. In using the book read it over and then follow the advice step by step. As Winston Churchill once said "the secret of good advice is to know when to take it." And how and what to do with it.

Chapter 2. Giving Nervousness the Quietus [the fatal stroke]

Even the most experienced public speaker will feel nervousness when taken out of his milieu, when the audience is larger, or more critical, or when the stakes are very high. What follows is a recipe for minimizing nervousness:

1. Be prepared. Have your speech written [at least on note cards] and rehearse it at least once, preferably twice. If it is impromptu, mentally rehearse the opening while being introduced. Keep the note cards on the podium.
2. Pick a date and a time that will find you rested. NEVER APPEAR WITH ANY INJURY OR BANDAGE.
3. Visit where the speech is to be held, before you speak, [more on why later]
4. If it is a cocktail hour function consume no more than one drink containing a maximum of 3 oz. of 80 proof alcohol.
5. Do not bring any family members if it can be avoided.
6. Dress appropriately to the event.
7. Dress using the appropriate color scheme. More on what is appropriate, later as well.
8. Above all beforehand seize every opportunity to practice speaking. Your ability to perform before an audience is like a muscle, the only way to avoid flabbiness is to practice, exercising your skills over and over.
9. The more you do number 8, the less nervous you will be.
10. Use the psychological concept of primacy/ recency in your speech.

What will follow is an elaboration of how to do these things and the reasons I have selected them. Detailed examples from historical speaking events and from my own experience illustrate these lessons.

Chapter 3. Be Prepared. The Do's of effective speech writing.

Just like in sex, in speaking length matters, only unlike sex in which it may be best to be a "60 minute man" or woman, in speech, shorter is better. One of the great poems of the English language is very short but very expressive. Lord Byron had a lover named Caroline Lamb which he drilled with vigor and in many romantic places, their relationship was tempestuous and scandalous. Byron aptly and succinctly immortalized the bittersweet relationship with a many faceted limerick, " Caroline Lamb, God Damn." From this we can conclude she must have had many talents, hidden and public, good and bad.

St. Thomas Aquinas, reportedly said "if you can't save a soul in 20 minutes it can't be saved," and this is borne out by modern research which now sets 18 to 20 minutes as the ideal length of a speech for today's audiences. Barry Goldwater's entire campaign for president was blown out of the water by a one minute ad in 1964, "Daisy Girl." Dan Quayle was finished off by Senator Lloyd Benson, by one well delivered cutting remark. Brevity is the soul of wit.

Abraham Lincoln was reportedly asked about why his Gettysburg address was so short, and replied, "If I'd had more time, I would have said less." As Lincoln's address [and Byron's limerick] illustrates,   deep meaning can be conveyed in very little time. Lincolns Gettysburg address at the most takes 3 minutes to deliver, yet the intense meaning is fully conveyed. So intense is the message, that it is truly timeless. The lesson is keep it brief; you want to emotionally move your audience, not drown them with empty words.

One of the key concepts in effective speech writing is to use words that pierce the psyche, by evoking emotion. A logical appeal must be followed by an emotional one, and when in doubt, always choose emotion over logic. An example of how this works is taken form an opening argument in a wrongful termination case. The wrong way to do this would be: " This case is about the termination of my client's employment and arises under the DFEH and 42 USC 2000 e et seq., for which my client seeks damages." This is dull and un persuasive. The correct way to do it is: " This case is about the brutal and callous termination of Jose Mayo, an award winning salesman, who for twenty years had turned in award winning sales, despite having to endure an overwhelmingly oppressive environment replete with repeated prolonged vicious public tongue lashings, constant soul numbing humiliation and racial harassment dished out with obvious relish for more than two decades the hands of his boss, a cruel, cunning, conniving, brutal bigot ." Now, which description captured your interest?

Some famous examples of piercing and emotional verbal descriptions are very short. Former Vice President John Nance Garner when asked what the Vice Presidency was worth replied, "The Vice Presidency isn't worth a pitcher of warm piss." That certainly says what Vice President Garner thought with stunning clarity. This was later cleaned up to "spit" so it could be printed in the New York Times.

Some of my personal speech students really absorbed this lesson. Beau Wilding, who also took English from me after Speech when I asked Beau after I showed "A Streetcar Named Desire" [in which Marlon Brando goes through the play wearing "wife beaters" flexing his biceps and punching out his wife,] what Beau thought was the main message of the play was, could have said: " The author wanted to demonstrate that some women are attracted to lower class bullying men." Instead, Beau replied; " Nice guys don't get laid." Colorful, short and to the point, this still is the most pungent analysis of this play I have ever heard, proving once again, brevity is the soul of wit.

Franklin Roosevelt was a master at using words that conveyed emotion. On May 7, 1933, during the Banking crises in one of his Fireside chats, during the "Height of the Depression" [my father's description of the era] when over 75% of the homeowners were foreclosed on FDR did not say that the economy had problems, he said…."The country is dying by inches." This leaves no doubt that the economy had cratered. Similarly in a war message to Congress December 9, 1941, President Roosevelt in words that resonate today [post 9/11]; "And what we have learned is this: There is no security for any nation or any individual in a world ruled by principles of gangsterism. There is no such thing as impregnable defense against powerful aggressors who sneak up in the dark and strike without warning." FDR did not call Pearl Harbor a "tragedy" it was a "day of infamy" a "sneak attack" he used words that were potent, not limp, he did not talk like a wimp. FDR knew how to harness emotion. Governor Schwarzenegger obviously knows this lesson and knows when to label opponents "Girlie men" and when not to for persuasive effect.

Sometimes emotion is the only way to overcome a cruel cold logical calculus. The late Moe Green [what better name for a personal injury lawyer, just think if they asked the client who your lawyer was, what the name itself says] Moe once was asked how to overcome the insurance tables which ask a jury to value a life strictly by the earning capacity and or history of the victim. Under such formulas poor people, children and old people have little economic value, they are cheap road pizza. In this case a bag lady had been run over and killed by a city bus. Her husband was also homeless and faced the world with a shopping cart and plastic bags after sleeping on a bus bench and had done so for years. Their earnings were squat. They were both in their seventies. The defendant bus company was going to argue the loss to the husband of his wife should be calculated by the statutory tables and thus would amount to a pittance. Moe constructed his argument as follows: " Now in this case the defendants will say my client's wife earned very little and so he lost very little. This is not the case. When a multi-millionaire loses a million dollars, he has lost a lot, but he is still a rich man, if you have ten million and lose one you still have nine million. But what did the defendants take from Mr. Jones? The defendants took from him ALL that he had. ALL Mr. Jones had in this world, was his wife. Who now will cook for him? Who now will be his companion? Who now will give him warmth, comfort and affection in the winter of his life? The loss is so much greater when the defendants, by carelessly running over and killing his wife like a stray dog in the street, took forever from a poor man, all he had." Now does that emotional appeal make you want to value the bag lady's life differently? This is why they paid Moe Green.

You can think now of other examples. But the lesson is clear, use colorful clear, emotionally loaded words, otherwise your speech will not be worth a "pitcher of warm piss."

4. Primacy Recency

So now you are marshalling your adjectives in Churchillian squads expending much " Blood, sweat, tears, and toil." to make your speech penetrate your audience. So how do you begin and end your speech? With a bang! Primacy Recency is a psychological phenomenon that has established that what an audience [or any listener] remembers most is what they hear and see first and last. So you need to begin your speech [briefing, presentation, etc.] with a bang and end with one.

This is even more important because recent studies of sales have concluded that trust is established within 30 seconds to two minutes. It is established by both verbal and physical signals. It is best illustrated by the famous Kennedy-Nixon Debates. Most instructive is the first debate, it is the most instructive because it was the most decisive of the debates. Tapes of this are available from several sources on the web. To get the most from this chapter you should buy one and watch it, to see what I am saying.

Prior to the debates Kennedy in the Gallup polls was running behind. He was a Catholic and large areas of the country were still in the throes of anti-Catholic propagandists, like Gerald L.K. Smith. Nixon had been Vice President and was using an effective campaign slogan, "Experience Counts" and had been on TV and in the press for years. Most analysts today have concluded that Nixon should never have agreed to debate. But he did and his mistakes gave his campaign the fatal stroke. Historians have concluded that Nixon could have won the debates and the election had he not blundered. Hubris perhaps played a part, Nixon was an attorney and had debated often in the House. He did have a lot of debating experience, he probably underestimated his opponent and did not practice

Primacy recency has many facets. One of them is illustrated by Nixon's first mistake. Nixon was offered the chance to speak first, he declined and Kennedy readily accepted. By going first Kennedy had the chance to immediately give the first impression to the audience. By throwing the first "pitch" so to speak, Kennedy had the priceless chance to sell the voters so strongly that nothing thereafter would change their minds. Going first gained Kennedy primacy recency in the debate.

Nixon also had unwittingly violated rule 7 he did not dress in the right color. Always dress to contrast as much as possible with the background. Nixon wore a gray suit. Kennedy's team knew that the background was gray and dressed in a dark blue suit that his team knew would make him stand out, especially on TV. [This is also true in live performance]

A digression on Kennedy's preparations. Kennedy's team had decided at the outset of the primaries to use all that was known about image enhancement. Warner Brother's studios via Jack Warner lent some of their expertise. It was decided that both Jack and Jacqueline Kennedy would have custom designed clothes [the famous two button suit and her pillbox hat] so that whenever their picture was taken they would look their best. The press and TV were all black and white so the colors chosen generally were picked to look best in black and white photographs. They were actors in a large moving picture the campaign.

Moreover they knew the lesson research has confirmed appearance counts, so both worked out like prizefighters to be in shape. The late John Derek once summed up this harsh truth, " appearance is everything, I never would have had the jobs I have had or the women I have had [notably Bo Derek] if it were not for the way I looked." Even the infamous Adolph Hitler once said " it is difficult to deliver a dynamic speech if you are fat."

Nixon then made big mistake three, Kennedy had also dress rehearsed the debates in secret and knew that he was tanned, fit and well dressed, he knew from his own filmed/taped rehearsals that he did not need makeup. So when Don Hewlitt the CBS producer offered makeup to Kennedy, he declined, Nixon not wanting to be out macho'd also declined and was given only a perfunctory makeup job. It and Nixon looked so bad Hewlitt had the Republican advisor to Nixon look through the camera and give the ok to proceed, and the advisor agreed. Nixon had injured his leg, had been in the hospital was on antibiotics and was still ill when the event took place. Nixon always had heavy stubble and as the event progressed began to perspire on his upper lip. The ill look could have been remedied by a good makeup job.

Thus Nixon blundered the event away. The contrast between him and the tanned fit, contrastingly dressed Kennedy was so powerful that Nixon's message was lost, submerged in a sea of errors. Moreover Nixon compounded the appearance factor by the way he sat, often knock need, which gave him an oddball appearance, Kennedy on the other hand sat straight with his legs appropriately crossed.

Kennedy also ended strongly, reminding voters that his was the party of "Franklin Roosevelt and the New Deal" even though I watched the debate at the time and several times since I cannot remember Nixon's ending. He did not end with a bang.

This event tellingly illustrates primacy recency as well as all the best approaches to any public event. Scout the place you will speak so you can contrast with the background. [This is not always possible but make every effort] Be in the best shape you can and always go first if you can. Always begin with a strongly phrased introduction and finish equally strongly. Start with a bang and end with a bang.

Later studies showed those that only listened to the debate on radio thought Nixon won. This confirmed the decisive role of appearance. The effect on the campaign was decisive, Kennedy became a star, large crowds now attended every event, he surged in the polls and went on to victory. Nixon went on to make a comeback by learning the lessons of this series of blunders. Nixon never violated any of these rules again and life gave Nixon a second chance. Life does not always give anyone a second chance so this book is to help you be prepared for your first and possibly only chance.

Just to show that the technique has ancient antecedents, one of its most effective uses was in Ancient Greece. One of history's great lawyers was Pericles, [possibly known as Moe Drachma] he was defending a young maiden charged with heresy and for which the penalty was death. The trial took place before an all male jury. In concluding his closing argument for the defense Pericles said, "Finally we must see that a woman of such beauty is herself a gift from the Gods, and to squander such beauty by putting her to death would in itself be an act of profound heresy." And as he spoke those final words he removed the top of her toga to reveal what history records as two of the most beautiful breasts ever given to a European woman, full, pink, perky and persuasive. With exhibits A and B in full view, the all male jury unanimously returned a verdict of not guilty on the spot. Thus ancient advocates knew full well how to end with a bang.

5. Pick a date and a time that will find you rested. NEVER APPEAR WITH ANY INJURY, BANDAGE or CAST.

As any permanently disfigured person will tell you, the public has an intense subconscious and conscious dislike of the injured. Franklin Roosevelt would never be elected President today because our vicious, shallow, callow, poltroonistic media would have displayed FDR in his wheelchair. In his time the media was a profession that had some moral responsibility and interest in the public and personal interest of humanity and never printed a picture of FDR in his wheelchair.

Despite all of our spin for the disabled this is an iron law that must never be broken by the speaker. What follows is an example from my true personal experience which illustrates this lesson as well as why I had to re learn earlier lessons in speech and why I am a believer that repetition is the soul of learning as anyone who knows the rest of the phrases "Built like a _____." Or Winston tastes good ...." Or see the USA in your_____.

 A personal illustration of why you should never appear when you are obviously in injured or ill follows In 1987 I made a startling discovery while getting ready to attend the AALS teacher hiring fair. I discovered that my alma mater "The Stanford Law School" had intentionally or carelessly sabotaged my early career probably costing me over a million dollars, and eliminating the possibility of a good beginning to my legal career. After much unrelenting toil, tears and sweat, I had graduated from there in 1975. But a strange thing happened, I could not get a job. I graduated unemployed. I had always concluded that this was due to two factors, that 1974-76 was the deepest recession since 1929 and anti Hispanic bias. One on campus interviewer had said that " Dave why should I hire you when I can get another attorney with the same credentials and never worry about alienating any clients? So I looked no deeper.

I remained unemployed as a Lawyer until late 1976. I can really relate to those who lived through the Great Depression. I can still see through the veil of years my late mother and my wife in our old living room wondering why I was having such trouble getting a job. Wherever I sent my resume cover letter and transcripts to I got a rejection. The transcripts were always sent directly from the school, I still had my copy of my grades and always relied on the school sending the official transcripts. I still recall the late nights sending out these three or four a night to no avail. [This was pre word processor, these were done on a typewriter with carbon copies] The only job I got was on a hunch. I walked into a Public defenders office and talked my way into a job I knew nothing about defending CRIMINAL clients that still make my skin crawl. I had prepared to be a Real estate or UCC transactional attorney. I did not take any trial advocacy courses, though they had been available. Though I won my first two jury trials, overall I did poorly in a job I was learning on the fly. It took years for my career to semi recover. Five years later, 1981, I got my first job as a Real estate attorney at a third rate firm earning wages below the market.

In 1987 I discovered by ordering a transcript sent to myself that Stanford Law School had inserted into my OFFICIAL GRADUATE TRANSCRIPT an incomplete in Freshman English and other grades that did not belong to me, but in fact belonged to another David M. Ramirez they had admitted as an undergraduate! A true copy of this erroneous transcript is attached. This is when I began to smell the roses with regard to my early career. Stanford in its most official statement about me said to all those employers that I as a graduate student could not pass bonehead English. This played into the hands of the worst stereotypes that the public has about Hispanic's, that we all speak with an accent and cannot write in English. The truth is that I never took any

15

English class at Stanford. My first two years were spent at a superior institution Cal State Fullerton, where I tested into college English IA and did such a good job [thanks to my high school teachers Mr. Cook and Mrs. Evelyn Talbott] that I was nominated for College Honors English, in which I earned B as I came out of a hospital bed from a near fatal car accident and took the final while suffering from the remains of a concussion.

Other consequences had ensued. One employer General Dynamic's even sent me to a remedial English class in 1978-79. [I had gotten a job as a contract administrator as all they required was a BA.] You may ask why didn't you order you own official transcript earlier? Having come from a State College, I did not because the State college would not send an official transcript to the student. In fact the envelope said if they delivered one to you in person "un official if opened" Stanford followed a similar policy, and I had my copy of the report cards.

Naturally I was angry. I called and immediately wrote my alma mater and demanded the transcript be corrected. A meeting was held with me, Sally Mahoney, the registrar whose office had done this and Fernando De Necochea an assistant to the University president. This meeting resulted in my transcript being semi corrected [they did delete the undergraduate grades from my graduate transcript] and a half hearted effort was made to make amends by Stanford. Fernando wrote a lukewarm letter of support for my candidacy to become a law professor. What was not half hearted was the agreement of the late John Kaplan to be a reference for the AALS job conference. I did not know he was dying at the time and always considered he was the best teacher I ever saw in action at any level, any time. I had first seen him debate the late Joe Pyne, an early shock TV host and took every class he ever offered. He opened his undergraduate class in law with the Queen vs. Dudly and Stevens, an event I still recall.

This meeting resulted in an invitation to talk about continuing guarantees to Notre Dame Law School as part of interviewing for a job. It was for me to be a defining moment.

Just prior to the speech I broke my foot. I shattered three bones in my right foot. I had a cast from the knee down with a walking rubber sole. I was supposed to use crutches, but I decided that with sheer grit I could do without. Prescription pain killers eased the pain and I decided to stop the pain killers the night before the event so my thinking would be clear for the post speech questions. I also brought my wife as she was going to have to move if I got the job. She was seated in the audience.

The pain killer wore off about thirty minutes before the event. Now I had a shooting excruciating pain that shot straight through me whenever I tried to put any weight on my foot at all. I limped an am sure grimaced as I went to the podium. I began ad used my notes, I attempted to stand straight, and every time I did the pain was excruciating so I altered my stance, and I am sure that the audience saw a slight rocking as I moved from foot to foot. Within three minutes, my audience began to interrupt with some very tough questions, and with the increase in pain as the event went on as well as the increase of tension, I began a la Nixon in 1960 to sweat. If I noticed sweat on my upper lip and brow, it had to be noticeable to the very discerning audience of Notre Dameistas. Then as I grappled with a tough question, the Dameista faculty struck like Presa Canarieo dogs after a steak. Questions came in rapid fire. I waffled and fumbled my way through the rest of the talk. I am sure I looked like a combination of Commander Stockdale in his Vice presidential debate, Barry Goldwater during his speech televised when he was ill, and me at my worst. I literally melted down out there. It was my worst day ever on a public platform. I remember when I stepped outside in the 30 degree weather, steam came off of me.

Needless to say, not only did no job offer result, but the stigma of bombing out still may remain. In the early 1990's I interviewed for a job marketing CEB seminars with CEB, aka California Continuing Education of the Bar. I did well and advanced to the final round. [I had by this time relearned the skills set forth in this book and attach the evaluations of my presentations as an exhibit] When I got to the final interviewer, a sixty five year old white man with beady blue narrow set eyes, he looked at me as though I were something on the bottom of his shoe and said " I remember you, you're the guy who melted down at Notre Dame." I did not get that job either.

This series of events was defining for me. The flop at Notre Dame inspired me to re teach myself and inspired this book.

As I examine the Notre Dame event, it did re teach some key lessons. NEVER appear injured, ever. From reports on NPR Saddam Hussein has a ruptured disc in his back which causes him to limp whenever he has to walk more than ten yards. He is NEVER videoed walking more than ten feet and never with a limp. Learning from Hitler, who had special typewriters built to type his notes in ¾ inch high letters so he would never be seen wearing glasses, Sadam has his speeches in 24 point type on a teleprompter. Never display any sign of physical weakness. FDR did not and you should not either, ever.

Never bring any relative to an event if it can be avoided. Recent studies have proven that in unfamiliar settings you do better totally among strangers.

If you have not spoken in a while, be sure you practice in front of a live audience first, any live audience. Speech is like a muscle, and the only way to perfect the skill is to do it, whether it is with a church group or with a highs school or other group.

6. Repetition is the soul of learning and the link and primacy recency.

The classic example of the mix of primacy recency along with repetition and the link are the speeches of Scipio the elder a Roman Senator during the time of the Punic Wars between Rome and Carthage. He always concluded in his best and strongest voice, each and every speech with the phrase " Carthage must be destroyed." And ultimately Carthage was destroyed.

This was the use of all three concepts. Remember primacy recency says that the mind remembers beginnings and endings thus you should start and end in a memorable way, repetition means just that that which is repeated will be remembered. American advertising is sure proof of the concept. Many slogans have been repeated so often that to those exposed they are automatically remembered. For example "Like a rock." Relates to what car? I wish I were an Oscar Meyer Weiner...........can you finish the rest? Winston tastes good like a.........can you finish this one? See the USA in you're.............? Or for those from LA "11980 East Firestone........... Repetition works even though it is pooh poohed by all the trendy politically correct educators as not a good teaching technique, it really works. Sixty years after World War II many Americans who were alive then can tell you the end of this slogan " Loose lips............ and many Germans alive during the Hitler tyranny can give the end of this slogan " Ein Volk, Ein Reich, Ein.........By the way what coffee is "good to the very last drop?"

It was an American advertising agency that discovered the uses of the link, the originator was a psychologist employed in marketing to sell shampoo. The shampoo was always linked with the picture of a woman with long blond hair. He advised always linking the brand of the shampoo with a picture of a woman with long blond hair.

The process requires repetition but this actual use proved that it works.

An example of the most successful link is the Marlborough Man. Over 50 years ago the brand was a poor seller. It was a nondescript brand with no real following. But following earlier uses of the link, Uncle Ben with rice and a long haired Blond with white rain shampoo the ad agency decided to link Marlborough with a rugged masculine looking cowboy on horseback. The first one was a former New York Giants quarterback who looked every inch the part, Charley Connerly. The principal of the link is association, every time the package of the product is shown it was shown with the picture of the rugged manly cowboy on horseback. The brand Marlborough after years and years of millions of repetitions now brings into your mind that picture of the rugged cowboy just with the mere mention of the products name. The picture also brings with it all of the positive tough guy associations, and thus lighting up a Marlborough makes the "macho guy" statement, all by virtue of the linkage of one association with another.

Just to give credit where it is due the link is really just an extension of Pavlov's work. As you recall Pavlov associated feeding dogs with a bell. After many many repetitions he discovered that just by ringing the bell the dogs would salivate so strong was the association. The extension is that the link is extending the association to a different type of association, instead of a bell to a picture or other event.

Another example of an extension of the link and its interplay with repetition is the work of the US Army in combat marksmanship and in martial arts and other forms of education and training.

During WW II, the combat debriefing and study of actual combat experience discovered that in combat less than on third of the soldiers who were in range actually fired at the enemy. It was discovered that in most humans there is a natural and or societal reluctance to shoot to kill other people.

Only a decided minority naturally possessed the killer instinct to repeatedly and successfully shoot to kill as many of the enemy as rapidly as possible. This was gruesomely confirmed by the experience of Stalin's NKVD and the SS Einsatzgruppen, who actually had to be relieved and rotated out after months of machine gunning helpless disarmed civilians.

Consequently a method was needed to increase the combat shooting percentage to over 90%. The theory was that if this level of combat shooting could be achieved the Army would be far more efficient resulting in shorter wars which would mean fewer US deaths overall. After all Patton was right, you do not win wars by dying for your country, but by making the other poor dumb son of a bitch die for his, and in wholesale numbers. The method that has been proven to work uses repetition and the link. It was discovered that if the soldier was trained to perform a set of activities [i.e. taking aim and firing] which was linked to a pop up of a human silhouette and repeated this thousands of times, that sometime after the 2000th repetition whenever the human silhouette appeared the soldier would automatically fire at the silhouette. The desired behavior would take place without thinking and would override any natural inhibition against the behavior that the soldier possesses. All the firing ranges were changed to feature pop up targets with human silhouettes. Combat firing rates increased to over 90%.

This also was applied to martial arts. In this area it was discovered that there was a natural reluctance to apply the fatal stroke to the opponent in hand to hand combat. Clearly in war where the mission is to kill the enemy, to survive the soldier should have no hesitation in administering the quietus [what the Romans called the release of death] to the enemy. Again repetition was the solution. In hand to hand combat after two thousand drills at administering the fatal stroke the action became automatic.

This automatic response effect of repetition is now so well proven that it has even been used in court to successfully defend a murder case. In one case reported in the L.A. Times a former South Vietnamese ranger was sent from a reunion celebration in Garden Grove to buy some Courvoisier XO cognac. According to the witnesses cited in the newspaper account, when the five foot five Ranger went in [as was apparently his habit] he was carrying a loaded 45 caliber semi-automatic US Army issue Colt pistol. The ARVN Ranger calmly picked up the XO and went to the counter to pay. At the counter he was confronted by a young jealous, big brutal Anglo bigot who must have had a cranium only two fingers high. "What's a gook like you doing buying expensive cognac like that" The ARVN Ranger said nothing and simply placed the two hundred dollars on the counter. The bullying Anglo bigot came out from behind the counter and shoved the ARVN Ranger "Why don't you go back to Vietnam?" Still no response from the ARVN ranger. The six foot two vicious Anglo bigot then punched the ARVN Ranger flooring him. When the ARVN Ranger got up in one single move he hit the bully in the solar plexus decking the bully and when the Anglo hit the floor rolling onto his back the ARVN Ranger pulled the 45 Colt pistol, placed it in the center of the bigot's chest and emptied the magazine. Witnesses said that with each round the body bounced off the ground into the muzzle. When the magazine was empty the ARVN Ranger calmly placed the pistol in his holster and waited for the police.

At his trial for first degree murder the former ARVN Ranger testified that he had been extensively trained and when he was punched it set off an automatic reaction which is why he continued to fire until he had emptied the magazine. The court also allowed expert testimony about automatic responses. For this to occur meant that the court found that the scientific basis for such a theory was sufficiently established to allow expert testimony on the subject. The jury found that indeed the punch triggered the automatic response and that since it was unthinking the ARVN ranger did not have the specific intent [the premeditated killing of a human being with malice aforethought] to commit murder, and he was acquitted.

There are many lessons for the speaker from this proven theory. Among the lessons from this is that repetition does work, so it should be used often in speech. Secondly that the more you speak the more automatic your response will be to the situation. Thirdly you can create a positive atmosphere by use of the link.

Two of the best known examples of early linkage are the campaign songs of Franklin Delano Roosevelt and Adolph Hitler. When Happy Days Are Here Again is played, anyone who knows of the era automatically thinks of the smiling FDR at a campaign rally. Hitler used "Ride of the Valkyries" as a pre speech warm up so often that after WW II Wagner's works were banned from public exhibition in Germany for many years as being Nazi music. Similarly many orchestras and symphony groups would not play Wagner because of the Nazi associations it would bring to mind.

Entertainers often made use of this link. Who do you think of when "Thanks for the Memories" is played, Ming the Merciless? Or "I left my Heart in San Francisco? Or "The Christmas Song" The point is that you can do the same if you or your company have a sales campaign.

Martin Luther King used repetition all the time within a speech. In one of his famous speeches He repeated " How long? And answered his own question ' Not long' until the audience took up the answer, "Not long." Academics denigrate repetition as mindless, in some ways it is, but it is mindless in the best way because it actually works, and works so well the response can be automatic, so long as the repetition is carried on long enough. After all who can forget, " Where's the _____."

The effectiveness of repetition and the link are so well documented that it is solid evidence that violent video games should be banned from sale to those under 21, and so should saturation TV coverage of lunatic mass murderers.

One of the reasons I have concluded that this needs to be done is simply reflecting on History. From 1776 until 1968 anyone in America could order firearms through the mail. There were no age or other restrictions you could buy shotguns and rifles and pistols semi automatic or conventional, from Sears and Wards among others. The founders also knew that freedom was not and cannot be free when they adopted the Second Amendment to our constitution which guarantees the right to individually keep and bear arms. They had experienced English tyranny and knew that personal power to escape tyranny came from words or guns. How many school shootings or other mass shootings were there from 1776 to 1968? Very few.

Now fast forward to the introduction of two constantly repeated stimuli spread over the mass of young American minds since the introduction of Nintendo type games in the early 1980's and the adoption of the news media format of "if it bleeds it leads." How many mass shootings occurred? The increase is startling.

The answer is not to repeal the Second Amendment. It is to remove these negative stimuli from the public media. The media as an industry does not want you to know about or control its power. It is so powerful that even one film can result in deaths, much less from millions of repetitions. Two films prove this point, many decades apart. Birth of a Nation and Deerhunter.

Birth of a Nation was the first racial exploitation film and was responsible for hundreds of lynchings of blacks. Its central theme is that all Blacks want is power and to have intercourse with white women. That this would have an effect was shown by the race riots [whites against blacks] caused by the film of Jack Johnson beating the shit out of the incumbent white heavyweight Champion Jack Burns, so incendiary was this film that it was banned from exhibition by Congress.

Thus the producers of Birth of a Nation took precautions to insure they could put butts in the seats and generate rivers of cash, because they knew the likely effect of the film. They knew that President Woodrow Wilson was a bigot and that he had grown up in reconstruction Virginia. So they arranged a screening of the film for the president. He emerged from the screening announcing that that was the way it was and ultimately signed a letter stating " This is a film every American must see." [There is a historical debate on the issue but I believe the evidence supports this conclusion] Armed with this the film was released nationwide. In many cities where it was shown, whites actively lynched Blacks. The KKK which had been dormant even moribund for many years enjoyed a rebirth, using this film as a recruiting tool emerged from the 1920's with millions of members, and throughout the South whites would be able to murder blacks with such impunity that the first white man convicted for the murder of a black man in Texas since 1865 would not occur until 1999.

In the 1970's the film Deerhunter which featured stupid and masochistic Vietnam returnees playing Russian Roulette with the resulting fatal gunshot wound to the head repeatedly chillingly and gruesomely portrayed, resulted in an increase in fatal incidents with people playing Russian roulette. Hollywood however disclaimed any responsibility for playing on the sado masochistic fascination of the public for death. Later on Natural born Killers allegedly spawned its own imitators.

Given that a limited display of a film can result in violent activity, what effect could a video game have? Some are very effective at rewarding violent behavior thought repetition and the link. This was shown by just one of the school shooters in Mississippi in that case a 14 year old who had never handled a real pistol had been addicted to playing a video game in which the player uses a plastic video pistol and shoots at the screen, human characters appear and the player is rewarded highly for any hit, but gets an even greater psychic reward [points and a big display] for well placed head shots. The 14 year old embryonic criminal played, and played and played, repeating thousands of times the eye hand motions needed to become expert at delivering fatal head shots unthinkingly, to moving human targets. He then became disturbed and went to a school prayer meeting with a 22 stolen from his fathers locked gun cabinet. In the space of minutes he used the real pistol to kill 8 people, 7 of which he administered head shots to, just like the drill. This shows that such games should never be offered for sale to those under 21. Just Like pornography and alcohol there is no constitutional bar to banning the sale of such violent video games and movies to those under 21. Yet the millions made from them have kept the Congress from banning the real cause of such mass shootings. We truly often do have the finest government money can buy.

7. Visual Aids

It is clear that a stunning visual can really add punch to your opening and closing of your speech. The best recent examples of the use of visual aids are Secretary of State Colin Powell' s recent briefing to the UN on the reasons for invading IRAQ, Gen Norman Schwarzkopf's post Gulf War Briefing, and most of Ross Perot's 1992 infomercials or speeches. A picture is worth a 1000 words, get copies look at these and note that the most powerful photo's are placed in the beginning and the end to make use of primacy recency.

A visual aid does not have to be a fancy power point or overhead, it can be a drawing on a blackboard. To illustrate this point, a late night comic when asked about the Clinton impeachment hearings, which had featured Monica Lewinsky being drilled by a Clinton cigar, was silent for about 40 seconds while he drew a four foot cigar shape on a white board and them turned to the audience and said while gesturing with his left hand toward the drawing, "Well about the impeachment, you just have to say……….. close… but no cigar!"
One can only imagine after the hearings, if Clinton offered a visitor cigar from his humidor, that you'd have to have glass of scotch to dip it in before you fired it up.

Another example of how it can be used is from a driving under the influence case I tried in San Diego Municipal Court in 1980-81. In this case my client was a bricklayer who had spent the night in Tijuana Mexico partying and killing a gallon bottle of Ouzo. As he approached the U.S. border he still had the now empty gallon bottle on the seat. The guard told him pull over here. He drove 10 feet perfectly straight and was arrested for DUI. Given a breathalyzer he blew a 3.1, 3.2. He never wobbled, passed out or even left his feet.

During my cross exam of the police lab tech I got him to give me an estimate in ounces of how many you would have to consume in two hours, and his estimate was 28 ounces of 100 proof alcohol. During my cross exam of the arresting officer I got him to testify that my client did not pass out, leave his feet stumble or throw up all during his observation of him after his arrest.

During my closing argument I drew the outline of a whisky bottle on the board and I drew a line on it just below the neck, to represent 28 ounces. That was in the background as I argued pointing at the board…

Now we have a very reasonable doubt here ladies and gentlemen. The peoples own expert testified that a man of his height and weight would have to consume 28 ounces of 100 proof liquor in two hours or less to blow a 3.1, 3.2 on the machine.

But what does experience and common sense tell you. They tell you that anyone who consumed that much alcohol would be on their knees worshiping at the "porcelain urn" literally firing out of both ends. And after a prolonged bout of projectile vomiting he would have passed out.

But what does the evidence show? He never left his feet, never staggered, never vomited, in fact he drove in a straight line and never passed out! The people have the burden of proof, if the symptoms do not match what the machine read out, this means the machine must be wrong. If the machine is wrong was his blood alcohol over the limit at all. This ladies and gentlemen is a very real and substantial reasonable doubt, and in the event of a reasonable doubt, the court will instruct you, that you must acquit.

The jury was out for three days. In the middle of the third day the jury was coming back from lunch when the Judge [a white male, then about 38 not Dick Murphy] said in a loud stage whisper before the court reporter could enter the

room" Why is this jury taking so long to convict this guy?"
The judge knew that I could not make a good record that he
had said it and that there would be no funds for an appeal. I
believe he had the hots for the cute young white female
prosecutor and wanted her to win. The jury then came back
in less than 20 minutes with a conviction. So though this is a
lesson that sex conquers all, but for the Judge biased remarks
my hand drawn visual aid would have won the day.

8. Historical examples of great speeches

The following is a set of examples of great speeches they are chosen because they are in the public record and illustrate the use of the emotional appeal for good and evil purposes. Most are available on video. Study them, especially in conjunction with a video of the speeches and you will see illustrations of how the suggestions I have made here work in practice.

Billy Sunday's Famous "Booze" Sermon THE FAMOUS "BOOZE" SERMON This sermon is a sensational message and an example of Billy Sunday's opposition to the liquor trade, saloons, and alcohol consumption. Sunday Is credited with being one of the most influential advocates of Prohibition during 1920's in the USA. Billy Sunday (1862-1935), was a professional baseball player from 1883 to 1891 for Chicago, Pittsburgh, and Philadelphia teams. He was converted through the street preaching of Harry Monroe of the Pacific Garden Mission in Chicago. He left a $5,000 a year salary as a baseball player for a $75 a month salary for the previously evangelistic YMCA. One of his teammates reputedly said "When Billy couldn't pitch in the majors anymore, he just started pitching' something else." He was known for great phrases such as " If you turned hell upside down, it would say 'Made in Germany' on the bottom of it."

He practiced his delivery in front of a mirror until it was perfect. If you view his films you will see that he made great use of gestures. From 1893 to 1895 was associated with J. Wilbur Chapman. He was an evangelist from 1893 to 1935. It is estimated that over 300,000 people walked the "sawdust trail" to receive Jesus Christ as Savior and Lord. The sermon has been excerpted because it violated the rule of brevity, in the style of the times it was very long, although with the dramatic gestures and vocal variety [loud and soft high and low vocal tones] that were Billy's trademark his audience stayed with him.

Rev. Billy Sunday:

Here we have one of the strangest scenes in all the Gospels. Two men, possessed Of devils, confront Jesus, and while the devils are crying out for Jesus to leave them, he commands the devils to come out, and the devils obey the command of Jesus. The devils ask permission to enter into a herd of swine feeding on the hillside. This is the only record we have of Jesus ever granting the petition of devils, and he did it for the salvation of men.

Then the fellows that kept the hogs went back to town and told the peanut-brained, weasel-eyed, hog-jowled, beetle-browed, bull-necked lobsters that owned the hogs, that "a long-haired fanatic from Nazareth, named Jesus, has driven the devils out of some men and the devils have gone into the hogs, and the hogs into the sea, and the sea into the hogs, and the whole bunch is dead." And then the fat, fussy old fellows came out to see Jesus and said that he was hurting their business. A fellow says to me, "I don't think Jesus Christ did a nice thing." You don't know what you are talking about. Down in Nashville, Tennessee, I saw four wagons going down the street, and they were loaded with stills, and kettles, and pipes. "What's this?" I said. "United States revenue officers, and they have been in the moonshine district and confiscated the illicit stills, and they are taking them down to the government scrap heap.

Jesus Christ was God's revenue officer. Now the Jews were forbidden to eat pork, but Jesus Christ came and found that crowd buying and selling and dealing in pork, and confiscated the whole business, and he kept within the limits of the law when he did it. Then the fellows ran back to those who owned the hogs to tell what had befallen them and those hog-owners said to Jesus: "Take your helpers and hike. You are hurting our business." And they looked into the sea and the hogs were bottom side up, but Jesus said, "What is the matter?" And they answered," Leave our hogs and go." A fellow says it is rather a strange request for the devils to make, to ask permission to enter into hogs. I don't know, if I was a devil I would rather live in a good, decent hog than in lots of men. If you will drive the hog out you won't have to carry slop to him, so I will try to help you get rid of the hog. The hog bearing the name of booze.

"Have you no interest in manhood?" "We have no interest in that; just take your disciples and leave, for you are hurting our business."That is the attitude of the liquor traffic toward the Church, and State, and Government, and the preacher that has the backbone to fight the most damnable, corrupt institution that ever wriggled out of hell and fastened itself on the public. I am a temperance Republican down to my toes. Who is the man that fights the whisky business in the South? It is the Democrats! They have driven the business from Kansas, they have driven it from Georgia, and Maine and Mississippi and North Carolina and North Dakota and Oklahoma and Tennessee and West Virginia. And they have driven it out of 1,756 counties. And it is the rock-ribbed Democratic South that is fighting the saloon. They started this fight that is sweeping like fire over the "United States. You might as well try and dam Niagara Falls with toothpicks as to stop the reform wave sweeping our land. The Democratic party of Florida has put a temperance plank in its platform and the Republican party of every state would nail that plank in their platform if they thought it would carry the election. It is simply a matter of decency and manhood, irrespective of politics. It is prosperity against poverty, sobriety against drunkenness, honesty against thieving, heaven against hell. Don't you want to see men sober? Brutal, staggering men transformed into respectable citizens? "No," said a saloonkeeper, "to hell with men. We are interested in our business, we have no interest in humanity." After all is said that can be said upon the liquor traffic, its influence is degrading upon the individual, the family, politics and business, and upon everything that you touch in this old world. For the time has long gone by when there is any ground for arguments as to its ill effects. All are agreed on that point. There is just one prime reason why the saloon has not been knocked into hell, and that is the false statement that "the saloons are needed to help lighten the taxes." The saloon business has never paid, and it has cost fifty times more than the revenue derived from it.

Does the Saloon Help Business?
I challenge you to show me where the saloon has ever helped business, education,church, morals or anything we hold dear. The wholesale and retail trade in Iowa pays every year at least $500,000 in licenses. Then if there were no drawback it ought to reduce the taxation twenty-five cents per capita. If the saloon is necessary to pay the taxes, and if they pay $500,000 in taxes, it ought to reduce them twenty-five cents a head. But no, the whisky business has increased taxes $1,000,000 instead of reducing them, and I defy any whisky man on God's dirt to show me one town that has the saloon where the taxes are lower than where they do not have the saloon. I defy you to show me an instance. Listen! Seventy-five per cent of our idiots come from intemperate parents; eighty per cent of the paupers, eighty-two per cent of the crime is committed by men under the influence of liquor; ninety per cent of the adult criminals are whisky-made. The Chicago Tribune kept track for ten years and found that 53,556 murders were committed by men under the influence of liquor. Archbishop Ireland, the famous Roman Catholic, of St. Paul, said of social crime today, that "seventy-five per cent is caused by drink, and eighty per cent of the poverty." I go to a family and it is broken up, and I say, "What caused this?" Drink! I step up to a young man on the scaffold and say, "What brought you here?" Drink! Whence all the misery and sorrow and corruption? Invariably it is drink. Five Points, in New York, was a spot as near like hell as any spot on earth. There are five streets that run to this point, and right in the middle was an old brewery and the streets on either side were lined with grog shops. The newspapers turned a searchlight

on the district, and the first thing they had to do was to buy
the old brewery and turn it into a mission.

The Parent of Crimes
The saloon is the sum of all villainies. It is worse than war or
pestilence. It is the crime of crimes. It is the parent of crimes
and the mother of sins. It is the appalling source of misery
and crime in the land. And to license such an incarnate fiend
of hell is the dirtiest, low-down, damnable business on top of
this old earth. There is nothing to be compared to it. The
legislature of Illinois appropriated $6,000,000 in 1908 to take
care of the insane people in the state, and the whisky business
produces seventy-five per cent of the insane. That is what
you go down in your pockets for to help support. Do away
with the saloons and you will close these institutions. The
saloons make them necessary, and they make the poverty and
fill the jails and the penitentiaries. Who has to pay the bills?
The landlord who doesn't get the rent because the money
goes for whisky; the butcher and the grocer and the charitable
person who takes pity on the children of drunkards, and the
taxpayer who supports the insane asylums and other
institutions, " at the whisky business keeps full of human
wrecks. Do away with the cursed business and you will not
have to put up to support them. Who gets the money? The
saloonkeepers and the brewers, and the distillers, while the
whisky fills the land with misery, and poverty, and
wretchedness, and disease, and death, and damnation, and it
is being authorized by the will of the sovereign people. You
say that "people will drink anyway." Not by my vote. You
say, "Men will murder their wives anyway." Not by my vote.
"They will steal anyway." Not by my vote. You are the
sovereign people, and what are you going to do about it? Let
me assemble before your minds the bodies of the drunken
dead, who crawl away "into the jaws of death, into the mouth
of hell," and then out of the valley of the shadow of the drink
let me call the appertaining motherhood, and wifehood, and
childhood, and let their tears rain down upon their purple
faces. Do you think that would stop the curse of the liquor
traffic? No! No!

In these days when the question of saloon or no saloon is at the fore in almost every community, one hears a good deal about what is called "personal liberty."These are fine, large, mouth-filling words, and they certainly do sound first rate; but when you get right down and analyze them in the light of common old horse-sense, you will discover that in their application to the present controversy they mean just about this: " Personal liberty" is for the man who, if he has the inclination and the price, can stand up at a bar and fill his hide so full of red liquor that he is transformed for the time being into an irresponsible, dangerous, evil-smelling brute. But "personal liberty" is not for his patient, long-suffering wife, who has to endure with what fortitude she may his blows and curses; nor is it for his children, who, if they escape his insane rage, are yet robbed of every known joy and privilege of childhood, and too often grow up neglected, uncared for and vicious as the result of their surroundings and the example before them. "Personal liberty" is not for the sober, industrious citizen who from the proceeds of honest toil and orderly living, has to pay, willingly or not, the tax bills which pile up as a direct result of drunkenness, disorder and poverty, the items of which are written in the records of every police court and poorhouse in the land; nor is" personal liberty " for the good woman who goes abroad in the town only at the risk of being shot down by some drink-crazed creature. This rant about "personal liberty" as an argument has no leg to stand upon.

The Economic Side

Now, in 1913 the corn crop was 2,373,000,000 bushels, and it was valued at $1,660,000,000. Secretary Wilson says that the breweries use less than two per cent; I will say that they use two per cent. That would make 47,000,000 bushels, and at seventy cents a bushel that would be about $33,000,000. How many people are there in the United States? Ninety millions. Very well, then, that is thirty-six cents per capita. Then we sold out to the whisky business for thirty-six cents apiece - the price of a dozen eggs or a pound of butter. We are the cheapest gang this side of hell if we will do that kind of business. Now listen! Last year the income of the United States government, and the cities and towns and counties, from the whisky business was $350,000,000. That is putting it liberally. You say that's a lot of money. Well, last year the workingmen spent $2,000,000,000 for drink, and it cost $1,200,000,000 to care for the judicial machinery. In other words, the whisky business cost us last year $3,400,000,000. I will subtract from that the dirty $350,000,000 which we got, and it leaves $3,050,000,000 in favor of knocking the whisky business out on purely a money basis. And listen, we spend $6,000,000,000 a year for our paupers and criminals insane, orphans, feeble-minded, etc., and eighty-two per cent of our criminals are whisky-made, and seventy-five per cent of the paupers are whisky-made. The average factory hand earns $450 a year, and it costs us $1,200 a year to support each of our whisky criminals. There are 326,000 enrolled criminals in the United States and 80,000 in jails and penitentiaries. Three-fourths were sent there because of drink, and then they have the audacity to say the saloon is needed for money revenue. Never was there a baser lie. "But," says the whisky fellow, "we would lose trade; I heard my friend ex-Governor Hanly, of Indiana, use the following illustrations: "Oh, but," they say, "Governor, there is another danger to the local option, because it means a loss of market to the farmer. We are consumers of large quantities of grain in the manufacture of our products. If you drive us out of business you strike down that market and it will create a money panic in this country, such as you have never seen, if you do that." I might answer it by saying that less than two per cent of the grain produced in this country is used for that purpose, but I pass that by. I want to debate the merit of the statement itself, and I think I can demonstrate in ten minutes to any thoughtful man, to any farmer, that the brewer who furnishes him a market for a bushel of corn is not his benefactor, or the benefactor of any man, from an economic standpoint. Let us see. A farmer brings to the brewer a bushel of corn. He finds a market for it. He gets fifty cents and goes his way, with the statement of the brewer ringing in his ears, that the brewer is the benefactor. But you haven't got all the factors in the problem, Mr. Brewer, and you cannot get a correct solution of a problem without all the factors in the problem. You take the farmer's bushel of corn, brewer or distiller, and you brew and distill from it four and one-half gallons of spirits. I don't know how much he dilutes them before he puts them on the market. Only the brewer, the distiller and God know. The man who drinks it doesn't, but if he doesn't dilute it at all, he puts on the market four and a half gallons of intoxicating liquor, thirty-six pints. I am not going to trace the thirty-six pints. It will take too long. But I want to trace three of them and I will give you no imaginary stories plucked from the brain of an excited orator. I will take instances from the judicial pages of the Supreme Court and the Circuit Court judges' reports in Indiana and in Illinois to make my case. Several years ago in the city of Chicago a young man of good parents, good character, one Sunday crossed the street and entered a saloon, open against the law. He found there boon companions. There were laughter, song and jest and much drinking. After awhile, drunk, insanely drunk, his money gone, he was kicked into the street. He found his way across to his mother's home. He importuned her for money to buy more drink. She refused him. He seized from the sideboard a revolver and ran out into the street and with the expressed determination of entering the saloon and getting more drink, money or no money. His fond mother followed him into the street. She put her hand upon turn in a loving restraint. He struck it from him in anger, and then his sister came and added her entreaty in vain. And then a neighbor, whom he knew, trusted and respected, came and put his hand on him in gentleness and friendly kindness, but in an insanity of drunken rage he raised the revolver and shot his friend dead in his blood upon the street. There was a trial; he was found guilty of murder. He was sentenced to life imprisonment, and when the little mother heard the verdict - a frail little bit of a woman - she threw up her hands and fell in a swoon. In three hours she was dead.

In the streets of Freeport, Illinois, a young man of good family became involved in a controversy with a lewd woman of the town. He went in a drunken frenzy to his father's home, armed himself with a deadly weapon and set out for the city in search of the woman with whom he had quarreled. The first person he met on the public square in the city, in the daylight, in a place where she had a right to be, was one of the most refined and cultured women of Freeport. She carried in her arms her babe, motherhood and babyhood, upon the streets of Freeport in the day time, where they had a right to be, but this young man in his drunken insanity mistook her for the woman he sought and shot her dead upon the streets with her babe in her arms. He was tried and Judge Ferand, in sentencing him to life imprisonment said: "You are the seventh man in two years to be sentenced for murder while intoxicated." In the city of Anderson, you remember the tragedy in the Blake home. A young man came home intoxicated, demanding money of his mother. She refused it. He seized from the wood box a hatchet and killed his mother and then robbed her. You remember he fled. The officer of the law pursued him and brought him back. An indictment was read to him charging him with the murder of the mother who had given him his birth, of her who had gone down into the valley of the shadow of death to give him life, of her who had looked down into his blue eyes and thanked God for his life. And he said, "I am guilty; I did it all." And Judge McClure sentenced him to life imprisonment.

Now I have followed probably three of the thirty-six pints of the farmer's product of a bushel of corn and the three of them have struck down seven lives, the three boys who committed the murders, the three persons who were killed and the little mother who died of a broken heart. And now, I want to know, my farmer friend, if this has been a good commercial transaction for you? You sold a bushel of corn; you found a market; you got fifty cents; but a fraction of this product struck down seven lives, all of whom would have been consumers of your products for their life expectancy. And do you mean to say that is a good economic transaction to you?

38

That disposes of the market question until it is answered; let no man argue further.

More Economics

And say, my friends, New York City's annual drink bill is $365,000,000 a year, $1,000,000 a day. Listen a minute. That is four times the annual output of gold, and six times the value of all the silver mined in the United States. And in New York there is one saloon for every thirty families. The money spent in New York by the working people for drink in ten years would buy every working man in New York a beautiful home, allowing $3,500 for house and lot. It would take fifty persons one year to count the money in $1 bills, and they would cover 10,000 acres of ground. That is what the people in New York dump into the whisky hole in one year. And then you wonder why there is poverty and crime, and that the country is not more prosperous.

The whisky gang is circulating a circular about Kansas City, Kansas. I defy you to prove a statement in it. Kansas City is a town of 100,000 population, and temperance went into effect July 1, 1905. Then they had 250 saloons, 200 gambling hells and 60 houses of ill fame. The population was largely foreign, and inquiries have come from Germany, Sweden and Norway, asking the influence of . the enforcement of the prohibitory law. At the end of one year the president of one of the largest banks in that city, a man who protested against the enforcement of the prohibitory law on the ground that it would hurt business, found that his bank deposits had increased $1,700,000, and seventy-two per cent of the deposits were from men who had never saved a cent before, and forty-two per cent came from men who never had a dollar in the bank, but because the saloons were driven out they had a chance to save, and the people who objected on the grounds that it would injure business found an increase of 209 per cent in building operations; and, furthermore, there were three times as many more people seeking investment, and court expenses decreased $25,000 in one year. Who pays to feed and keep the gang you have in jail? Why, you go down in your sock and pay for what the saloon has dumped in there. They don't do it. Mr. Whisky Man, why don't you go down and take a picture of wrecked and blighted homes, and of insane asylums, with gibbering idiots. Why don't you take a picture of that?

At Kansas City, Kansas, before the saloons were closed, they were getting ready to build an addition to the jail. Now the doors swing idly on the hinges and there is nobody to lock in the jails. And the commissioner of the Poor Farm says there is a wonderful falling off of old men and women coming to the Poor House, because their sons and daughters are saving their money and have quit spending it for drink. And they had to employ eighteen new school teachers for 600 boys and girls, between the ages of twelve and eighteen, that had never gone to school before because they had to help a drunken father support the family. And they have just set aside $200,000 to build a new school house, and the bonded indebtedness was reduced $245,000 in one year without the saloon revenue. And don't you know another thing: In 1906, when they had the saloon, the population, according to the directory, was 89,655. According to the census of 1907 the population was 100,835, or an increase of twelve per cent in one year, without the grogshop. In two years the bank deposits increased $3,930,000. You say, drive out the saloon and you kill business - Ha! Ha! "Blessed are the dead that die in the Lord."

I tell you, gentlemen, the American home is the dearest heritage of the people, for the people, and by the people, and when a man can go from home in the morning with the kisses of wife and children on his lips, and come back at night with an empty dinner bucket to a happy home, that man is a better man, whether white or black. Whatever takes away the comforts of home, whatever degrades that man or woman, whatever invades the sanctity of the home, is the deadliest foe to the home, to church, to state and school, and the saloon is the deadliest foe to the home, the church and the state, on top of God Almighty's dirt. And if all the combined forces of hell should assemble in conclave, and with them all the men on earth that hate and despise God, and purity, and virtue, if all the scum of the earth could mingle with the denizens of hell to try to think of the deadliest institution to home, to church and state, I tell you, sir, the combined hellish intelligence could not conceive of or bring an institution that could touch the hem of the garment of the open licensed saloon to damn the home and manhood, and womanhood, and business and every other good thing on God's earth. In the Island of Jamaica the rats increased so that they destroyed the crops, and they introduced a mongoose, which is a species of the coon. They have three breeding seasons a year and there are twelve to fifteen in each brood, and they are deadly enemies of the rats. The result was that the rats disappeared and there was nothing more for the mongoose to feed upon, so they attacked the snakes, and the frogs, and the lizards that fed upon the insects, with the result that the insects increased and they stripped the gardens, eating up the onions and the lettuce and then the mongoose attacked the sheep and the cats, and the puppies, and the calves and the geese. Now Jamaica is spending hundreds of thousands of dollars to get rid of the mongoose.

The American Mongoose

The American mongoose is the open licensed saloon. It eats the carpets off the floor and the clothes from off your back, your money out of the bank, and it eats up character, and it goes on until at last it leaves a stranded wreck in the home, a skeleton of what was once brightness and happiness. There were some men playing cards on a railroad train, and one fellow pulled out a whisky flask and passed it about, and when it came to the drummer he said, "No." "What," they said, "have you got on the water wagon?" and they all laughed at him- He said, "You can laugh if you want to, but I was born with an appetite for drink, and for years I have taken from five to ten glasses per day, but I was at; home in Chicago not long ago and I have a friend who has a pawn shop there. I was in there when in came a young fellow with ashen cheeks and a wild look on his face. He came up trembling, threw down a little package and said, 'Give me ten

41

cents.' And what do you think was in that package? It was a pair of baby shoes. "My friend said, 'No, I cannot take them. "But, he said, 'give me a dime. I must have a drink.' "'No, take them back home, your baby will need them.' "And the poor fellow said,' My baby is dead, and I want a drink.' " Boys, I don't blame you for the lump that comes up in your throat. There is no law, divine or human, that the saloon respects. Lincoln said, "If slavery is not wrong, nothing is wrong." I say, if the saloon, with its train of diseases, crime and misery, is not wrong, then nothing on earth is wrong. If the fight is to be won we need men - men that will fight - the Church, Catholic and Protestant, must fight it or run away, and thank God she will not run away, but fight to the last ditch. Who works the hardest for his money, the saloon man or you? Who has the most money Sunday morning, the saloon man or you?

The saloon comes as near being a rat hole for a wage-earner to dump his wages in as anything you can find. The only interest it pays is red eyes and foul breath,'and the loss of health. You can go in with money and you come out with empty pockets. You go in with character and you come out ruined. You go in with a good position and you lose it. You lose your position m the bank, or in the cab of tile locomotive. And it pays nothing back but disease and damnation and gives an extra dividend in delirium. tremens and a free pass to hell. And then it will let you, wife be buried in the potter's field, and your children go to the asylum, and yet you walk out and say the saloon is a good institution, when it is the dirtiest thing on earth. It hasn't one leg to stand on and has nothing to commend it to a decent man, not one thing. "But," you say, "we will regulate it by high license." Regulate what by high license? You might as well try and regulate a powder mill in hell. Do you want to pay taxes in boys, or dirty money? A man that will sell out to that dirty business I have no use for. See how absurd their arguments are. If you drink Bourbon in a saloon that pays $1,000 a year license, will it eat your stomach less than if you drink it in a saloon that pays $500 license? Is it going to have any different effect on you, whether the gang pays $500 or $1,000 license? No. It will make no difference whether you drink it over a mahogany counter or a pine counter, it will have the same effect on you; it will damn you. So there is no use talking about it.

In some insane asylums, do you know what they do? When they want to test some patient to see whether he has recovered his reason, they have a room with a faucet on in, and a cement floor, and they give the patient a mop and tell him to mop up the floor. And if he has sense enough to turn off the faucet and mop up the floor they will parole him, but should he let the faucet run, they know that he is crazy. Well, that is what you are trying to do. You are trying to mop it up with taxes and insane asylums and jails and Keeley cures, and reformatories. The only thing to do is to shut off the source of supply. A man was delivering a temperance address at a fair grounds and a fellow came up to him and said: "Are you the fellow that gave a talk on temperance?" "Yes.""Well, I think that the managers did a dirty piece of business to let you give a lecture on temperance. You have hurt my business and my business is a legal one."

"You are right there," said the lecturer, "they did do a mean trick; I would complain to the officers." And he took up a premium list and said: "By the way, I see there is a premium of so much offered for the best horse and cow and butter. What business are you in?" "I'm in the liquor business." "Well, I don't see that they offer any premium for your business. You ought t(? go down and compel them to offer a premium for your business and they ought to offer on the list $25 for the best wrecked home, $15 for the best bloated bum that you can show, and $10 for the finest specimen of broken-hearted wife, and they ought to give $25 for the finest specimens of thieves and gamblers you can trot out. You can bring out the finest looking criminals. If you have something that is good trot it out. You ought to come in competition with the farmer, with his stock, and the fancy work, and the canned fruit."

43

The Saloon a Coward

As Dr. Howard said: "I tell you that the saloon is a coward. It hides itself behind stained-glass doors and opaque windows, and sneaks its customers in at a blind door, and it keeps a sentinel to guard the door from the officers of the law, and it marks its wares with false bills-of-lading, and offers to ship green goods to you and marks them with the name of wholesome articles of food so people won't know what is being sent to you. And so vile did that business get that the legislature of Indiana passed a law forbidding a saloon to ship goods without being properly labeled. And the United States Congress passed a law forbidding them to send whisky through the mails. I tell you it strikes in the night. It fights under cover of darkness and assassinates the characters that it cannot damn, and it lies about you. It attacks defenseless womanhood and childhood. The saloon is a coward. It is a thief; it is not an ordinary court offender that steals your money, but it robs you of manhood and leaves you in rags and takes away your friends, and it robs your family It impoverishes your children and it brings insanity and suicide. It will take the shirt off your back and it will steal the coffin from a dead child and yank the last crust of bread out of the hand of the starving child; it will take the last bucket of coal out of your cellar, and the last cent out of your pocket, and will send you home bleary-eyed and staggering to your wife and children. It will steal the milk from the breast of the mother and leave her with nothing with which to feed her infant. It will take the virtue from your daughter. It is the dirtiest, most low-down, damnable business that ever crawled out of the pit of hell. It is a sneak, and a thief and a coward. It is an infidel. It has no faith in God; has no religion. It would close every church in the land. It would hang its beer signs on the abandoned altars. It would close every public school. It respects the thief and it esteems the blasphemer; it fills the prisons and the penitentiaries. It despises heaven, hates love, scorns virtue. It tempts the passions. Its music is the song of a siren. Its sermons are a collection of lewd, vile stories. It wraps a mantle about the hope of this world and that to come. Its tables are full of the vilest literature. It is the moral clearing house for rot, and damnation, and poverty, and insanity, and it wrecks homes and blights lives today.

God's Worst Enemy

The saloon is a liar. It promises good cheer and sends sorrow. It promises health and causes disease. It promises prosperity and sends adversity. It promises happiness and sends misery. Yes, it sends the husband home with a lie on his lips to his wife; and the boy home with a lie on his lips to his mother; and it causes the employee to lie to his employer. It degrades. It is God's worst enemy and the devil's best friend. . It spares neither youth nor old age. It is waiting with a dirty blanket for the baby to crawl into the world. It lies in wait for the unborn. It cocks the highwayman's pistol. It puts the rope in the hands of the mob. It is the anarchist of the world and its dirty red flag is dyed with the blood of women and children. It sent the bullet through the body of Lincoln; it nerved the arm that sent the bullets through Garfield and William McKinley. Yes, it is a murderer. Every plot that was ever hatched against the government and law, was born and bred, and crawled out of the grog-shop to damn this country. I tell you that the curse of God Almighty is on the saloon. Legislatures are legislating against it. Decent society is barring it out. The fraternal brotherhoods are knocking it out. The Masons and Odd Fellows, and the Knights of Pythias and the A. O. U. W. are closing their doors to the whisky sellers. They don't want you wriggling your carcass in their lodges. Yes, sir, I tell you, the curse of God is on it. It is on the down grade. It is headed for hell, and, by the grace of God, I am going to give it a push, with a whoop, for all I know how. Listen to me. I am going to show you how we burn up our money. It costs twenty cents to make a gallon of whisky; sold over the counter at ten cents a glass, it will bring four dollars. "But," said the saloonkeeper, "Bill, you must figure on the strychnine and the cochineal, arid other stuff they put in it, and it will bring nearer eight dollars."

Yes; it increases the heart beat thirty times more in a minute, when you consider the licorice and potash and logwood and other poisons that are put in. I believe one cause for the unprecedented increase of crime is due to the poison put in the stuff nowadays to make it go as far as they can. I am indebted to my friend, George B. Stuart, for some of the following points: I will show you how your money is burned up. It costs twenty cents to make a gallon of whisky, sold over the counter at ten cents a glass, which brings four dollars. Listen, where does it go? Who gets the twenty cents? The farmer for his corn or rye. Who gets the rest? The United States government for collecting revenue, and the big corporations, and part is used to pave our streets and pay our > police. I'll show you. I'm going to show you how it is burned up, and you don't need half sense to catch on, and if you don't understand just keep still and nobody will know the difference. I say, "Hey, Colonel Politics, what is the matter with the country?" He swells up like a poisoned pup and says to me, "Bill, why the silver bugbear. That's what is the matter with the country." The total value of the silver produced in this country in 1912 was $39,000,000. Hear me! In 1912 the total value of the gold produced in this country was $93,000,000, and we dumped thirty-six times that much in the whisky hole and didn't fill it. What is the matter? The total value of all the gold and silver produced in 1912 was $132,000,000, and we dumped twenty-five times that amount in the whisky hole and didn't fill it. What is the matter with the country, Colonel Politics? He swells up and says, "Mr. Sunday, Standpatism, sir." I say, "You are an old windbag." "Oh," says another, "revision of the tariff." Another man says, "Free trade; open the doors at the ports and let them pour the products in and we will put the trusts on the sidetrack." Say, you come with me to every port of entry. Listen! In 1912 the total value of all the imports was $1,812,000,000, and we dumped that much m the whisky hole in twelve months and did not fill it. "Oh," says a man, "let us court South America and Europe to sell our products. That's what is the matter; we are not exporting enough." Last year the total value of all the exports was $2,362,000,000, and we dumped that amount in the whisky hole in one year and didn't fill it. One time I was down in Washington and went to the United States treasury and said: "I wish you would let me go where you don't let the general public." And they took us around on the inside and we walked into a room about twenty feet long and fifteen feet wide and as many feet high, and I said, "What is this?" "This is the vault that contains all of the national bank stock in the United States." I said, "How much is here?" They said, "$578,000,000." And we dumped nearly four times the value of the national bank stock in the United States into the whisky hole last year, and we didn't fill the hole up at that. What is the matter? Say, whenever the day comes that all the Catholic and Protestant churches, just when the day comes when you will say to the whisky business: "You go to hell," that day the whisky business will go to hell. But you sit there, you old whisky-voting elder and deacon and vestryman, and you wouldn't strike your hands together on the proposition. It would stamp you an old hypocrite and you know it. Say, hold on a bit. Have you got a silver dollar? I am going to show you how it is burned up. We have in this country 250,000 saloons, and allowing fifty feet frontage for each saloon it makes a street from New York to Chicago, and 5,000,000 men, women and children go daily into the saloon for drink. And marching twenty miles a day it would take thirty days to pass this building, and marching five abreast they would reach 590 miles. There they go; look at them! On the first day of January, 500,000 of the young men of our nation entered the grog-shop and began a public career hellward, and on the 31st of December I will come back here and summon you people, and ring the bell and raise the curtain and say to the saloon and breweries: "On the first day of January, I gave you 500,000 of the brain and muscle of our land, and I want them back and have come in the name of the home and church and school; father mother, sister, sweetheart; give me back what I gave you. March out." I count, and 165,000 have lost their appetites and have become muttering, bleary-eyed drunkards, wallowing in their own excrement, and I say, "What is it I hear, a funeral dirge?" What is that procession? A funeral procession 3,000 miles long and 110,000 hearses in the procession. One hundred and ten thousand men die drunkards in the land of the free and home of the brave. Listen! In an hour twelve men die drunkards, 300 a day and 110,000 a year. One man will leap in front of a train, another will plunge from the dock into a lake, another will throw his hands to his head and life will end. Another will cry, "Mother," and his life will go out like a burnt match. I stand in front of the jails and count the whisky criminals. They say, "Yes, Bill, I fired the bullet." "Yes, I backed my wife into the corner and beat her life out. I am waiting for the scaffold; I am waiting." "I am waiting," says another, "to slip into hell." On, on, it goes. Say, let me summon the wifehood, and the motherhood, and the childhood and see the tears rain down the upturned faces. People, tears are too weak for that hellish business. Tears are only salty backwater that well up at the bidding of an occult power, and I will tell you there are 865,000 whisky orphan children in the United States, enough in the world to belt the globe three times around, punctured at every fifth point by a drunkard's widow. Like Hamilcar of old, who swore young Hannibal to eternal enmity against Rome, so I propose to perpetuate this feud against the liquor traffic until the white-winged dove of temperance builds her nest on the dome of the capitol of 'Washington and spreads her wings of peace, sobriety and joy over our land which I love with all my heart.

Huey Long's Senate Speeches

During his three brief years in the U.S. Senate, Huey Long became one of the most flamboyant and provocative Senators in the nation's history. He earned the enmity of his fellow Senators due to his frequent use of the filibuster to make some "point of principle" about which he was especially passionate, and due to his not infrequent habit of casting aspersions on the character of his fellow Senators. But the floor of the Senate gave Huey Long what he prized most, a bully pulpit from which to expound his views. He used this opportunity to the fullest--taking the Senate floor to place in the official record his arguments for his Share The Wealth program, and to proselytize for his general world-view. These speeches delivered during 1934 and 1935 make his case that the nation is in a mess and that his Share The Wealth program is the solution.By engaging in class warfare he nearly became President of the United States. To give some financial perspective, during the Height of the Depression, the U.S. Governments own checks were bouncing, the railroads only ran three days a week, vast numbers of Americans 30%to 40% were out of work and flat broke, shanty town's had sprung up all over the country, and for the "swells" the affluent who still had cash, a steak dinner with all the trimmings was thirty five cents. The country was on the verge of revolution.

THE CONGRESSIONAL RECORD -- February 5, 1934

Mr. Long: Mr. President, I send to the desk and ask to have printed in the RECORD not a speech but what is more in the nature of an appeal to the people of America. There being no objection, the paper entitled "Carry Out the Command of the Lord" was ordered to be printed in the RECORD, as follows:
By Huey P. Long, United States Senator People of America: In every community get together at once and

organize a share-our-wealth society--Motto: Every man a king

Principles and platform:
1. To limit poverty by providing that every deserving family shall share in the wealth of America for not less than one third of the average wealth, thereby to possess not less than $5,000 free of debt. 2. To limit fortunes to such a few million dollars as will allow the balance of the American people to share in the wealth and profits of the land. 3. Old-age pensions of $30 per month to persons over 60 years of age who do not earn as much as $1,000 per year or who possess less than $10,000 in cash or property, thereby to remove from the field of labor in times of unemployment those who have contributed their share to the public service. 4. To limit the hours of work to such an extent as to prevent overproduction and to give the workers of America some share in the recreations, conveniences, and luxuries of life. 5. To balance agricultural production with what can be sold and consumed according to the laws of God, which have never failed. 6. To care for the veterans of our wars. 7. Taxation to run the Government to be supported, first, by reducing big fortunes from the top, thereby to improve the country and provide employment in public works whenever agricultural surplus is such as to render unnecessary, in whole or in part, any particular crop.

Simple and Concrete--Not an Experiment
To share our wealth by providing for every deserving family to have one third of the average wealth would mean that, at the worst, such a family could have a fairly comfortable home, an automobile, and a radio, with other reasonable home conveniences, and a place to educate their children. Through sharing the work, that is, by limiting the hours of toil so that all would share in what is made and produced in the land, every family would have enough coming in every year to feed, clothe, and provide a fair share of the luxuries of life to its members. Such is the result to a family, at the

worst. From the worst to the best there would be no limit to opportunity.

One might become a millionaire or more. There would be a chance for talent to make a man big, because enough would be floating in the land to give brains its chance to be used. As it is, no matter how smart a man may be, verything is tied up in so few hands that no amount of energy or talent has a chance to gain any of it. Would it break up big concerns? No. It would simply mean that, instead of one man getting all the one concern made, that there might be 1,000 or 10,000 persons sharing in such excess fortune, any one of whom, or all of whom, might be millionaires and over.I ask somebody in every city, town, village, and farm community of America to take this as my personal request to call a meeting of as many neighbors and friends as will come to it to start a share-our-wealth society. Elect a president and a secretary and charge no dues. The meeting can be held at a courthouse, in some town hall or public building, or in the home of someone. It does not matter how many will come to the first meeting. Get a society organized, if it has only two members. Then let us get to work quick, quick, quick to put an end by law to people starving and going naked in this land of too much to eat and too much to wear. The case is all with us. It is the word and work of the Lord. The Gideons had but two men when they organized. Three tailors of Tooley Street drew the Magna Carta of England. The Lord says: "For where two or three are gathered together in My name, there am I in the midst of them." We propose to help our people into the place where the Lord said was their rightful own and no more. We have waited long enough for these financial masters to do these things. They have promised and promised. Now we find our country $10 billion further in debt on account of the depression, and big lenders even propose to get 90 percent of that out of the hides of the common people in the form of a sales tax. There is nothing wrong with the United States. We have more food than we can eat. We have more clothes and things out of which to make clothes than we can wear. We have more houses and lands than the whole 120 million can use if they all had good homes. So what is the trouble?

Nothing except that a handful of men have everything and the balance of the people have nothing if their debts were paid. There should be every man a king in this land flowing with milk and honey instead of the lords of finance at the top and slaves and peasants at the bottom.Now be prepared for the slurs and snickers of some high-ups when you start your local spread-our-wealth society. Also when you call your meeting be on your guard for some smart-aleck tool of the interests to come in and ask questions. Refer such to me for an answer to any question, and I will send you a copy. Spend your time getting the people to work to save their children and to save their homes, or to get a home for those who have already lost their own. To explain the title, motto, and principles of such a society I give the full information, viz: Title: Share-our-wealth society is simply to mean that God's creatures on this lovely American continent have a right to share in the wealth they have created in this country. They have the right to a living, with the conveniences and some of the luxuries of this life, so long as there are too many or enough for all. They have a right to raise their children in a healthy, wholesome atmosphere and to educate them, rather than to face the dread of their under-nourishment and sadness by being denied a real life. Motto: "Every man a king" conveys the great plan of God and of the Declaration of Independence, which said: "All men are created equal." It conveys that no one man is the lord of another, but that from the head to the foot of every man is carried his sovereignty. Now to cover the principles of the share-our-wealth society, I give them in order: 1. To limit poverty: We propose that a deserving family shall share in our wealth of America at least for one third the average. An average family is slightly less than five persons. The number has become less during depression. The United States total wealth in normal times is about $400 billion or about $15,000 to a family. If there were fair distribution of our things in America, our national wealth would be three or four or five times the $400 billion, because a free, circulating wealth is worth many times more than wealth congested and frozen into a few hands as is America's wealth. But, figuring only on the basis of wealth as valued when frozen into a few hands, there is the average of $15,000 to the family. We say that we will limit poverty of the deserving people. One third of the average wealth to the family, or $5,000, is a fair limit to the depths we will allow any one man's family to fall. None too poor, none too rich. 2. To limit fortunes: The wealth of this land is tied up in a few hands. It makes no difference how many years the laborer has worked, nor does it make any difference how many dreary rows the farmer has plowed, the wealth he has created is in the hands of manipulators. They have not worked any more than many other people who have nothing. Now we do not propose to hurt these very rich persons. We simply say that when they reach the place of millionaires they have everything they can use and they ought to let somebody else have something. As it is, 0.1 of 1 percent of the bank depositors nearly half of the money in the banks, leaving 99.9 of bank depositors owning the balance. Then two thirds of the people do not even have a bank account. The lowest estimate is that 4 percent of the people own 85 percent of our wealth. The people cannot ever come to light unless we share our wealth, hence the society to do it.

3. Old-age pensions:
Everyone has begun to realize something must be done for our old people who work out their lives, feed and clothe children and are left penniless in their declining years. They should be made to look forward to their mature years for comfort rather than fear. We propose that, at the age of 60, every person should begin to draw a pension from our Government of $30 per month, unless the person of 60 or over has an income of over $1,000 per year or is worth $10,000, which is two thirds of the average wealth in America, even figured on a basis of it being frozen into a few hands. Such a pension would retire from labor those persons who keep the rising generations from finding employment.

4. To limit the hours of work:
This applies to all industry. The longer hours the human family can rest from work, the more it can consume. It makes

no difference how many labor-saving devices we may invent, just as long as we keep cutting down the hours and sharing what those machines produce, the better we become. Machines can never produce too much if everybody is allowed his share, and if it ever got to the point that the human family could work only 15 hours per week and still produce enough for everybody, then praised be the name of the Lord. Heaven would be coming nearer to earth. All of us could return to school a few months every year to learn some things they have found out since we were there: All could be gentlemen: Every man a king. 5. To balance agricultural production with consumption: About the easiest of all things to do when financial masters and market manipulators step aside and let work the law of the Lord. When we have a supply of anything that is more than we can use for a year or two, just stop planting that particular crop for a year either in all the country or in a part of it. Let the Government take over and store the surplus for the next year. If there is not something else for the farmers to plant or some other work for them to do to live on for the year when the crop is banned, then let that be the year for the public works to be done in the section where the farmers need work. There is plenty of it to do and taxes of the big fortunes at the top will supply plenty of money without hurting anybody. In time we would have the people not struggling to raise so much when all were well fed and clothed. Distribution of wealth almost solves the whole problem without further trouble.

6. To care for the veterans of our wars: A restoration of all rights taken from them by recent laws and further, a complete care of any disabled veteran for any ailment, who has no means of support.

7. Taxation: Taxation is to be levied first at the top for the Governments support and expenses. Swollen fortunes should be reduced principally through taxation. The Government should be run through revenues it derives after allowing persons to become well above millionaires and no more. In this manner the fortunes will be kept down to reasonable size and at the same time all the works of the Government kept on a sound basis, without debts. Things cannot continue as they

now are. America must take one of three choices, viz: 1. A monarchy ruled by financial masters--a modern feudalism. 2. Communism. 3. Sharing of the wealth and income of the land among all the people by limiting the hours of toil and limiting the size of fortunes. The Lord prescribed the last form. It would preserve all our gains, share them among our population, guarantee a greater country and a happy people.

The need for such share-our-wealth society is to spread the truth among the people and to convey their sentiment to their Members of Congress. Whenever such a local society has been organized, please send me notice of the same, so that I may send statistics and data which such local society can give out in their community, either through word of mouth in meetings, by circulars, or, when possible, in local newspapers.

Please understand that the Wall Street controlled public press will give you as little mention as possible and will condemn and ridicule your efforts. Such makes necessary the organizations to share the wealth of this land among the people, which the financial masters are determined they will not allow to be done. Where possible, I hope those organizing a society in one community will get in touch with their friends in other communities and get them to organize societies in them. Anyone can have copies of this article reprinted in circular form to distribute wherever they may desire, or, if they want me to have them printed for them, I can do so and mail them to any address for 60 cents per hundred or $4 per thousand copies.

I introduced in Congress and supported other measures to bring about the sharing of our wealth when I first reached the United States Senate in January 1932. The main efforts to that effect polled about six votes in the Senate at first. Last spring my plan polled the votes of nearly twenty United States Senators, becoming dangerous in proportions to the financial lords. Since then I have been abused in the newspapers and over the radio for everything under the sun. Now that I am pressing this program, the lies and abuse in the big newspapers and over the radio are a matter of daily occurrence. It will all become greater with this effort. Expect that. Meantime go ahead with the work to organize a share-our-wealth society.

Sincerely,
  Huey P. Long,

THE CONGRESSIONAL RECORD -- January 23, 1935

MR. FRAZIER: Mr. President, I ask unanimous consent to have printed in the RECORD a radio address delivered by Senator HUEY P. LONG, of Louisiana, over the network of the National Broadcasting Co., of Washington, D.C., on January 19 last.

There being no objection, the address was ordered to be printed in the RECORD, as follows:

Our Growing Calamity

Ladies and gentlemen, the only means by which any practical relief may be given to the people is in taking the money with which to give such relief from the big fortunes at the top. The common people haven't anything worth having; and when you put a tax that falls on them for the purpose of unemployment relief or for old-age pensions, or for anything else, you are giving nobody any relief, because you are taxing the same people who have nothing, on the pretense that you are going to give it back to them. And s a matter of fact, it all never does get back, but much of it would remain in the hands of these Washington bureaucrats and politicians.

Now, we have been clamoring for a number of relief measures. Among them was the old-age pension. We did not propose any unreasonably high old-age pension as some other plans have suggested, but we did propose that every person who reached the age of 60 should receive something around from $30 to $40 per month. We excluded from the list all people who owned $10,000 worth of property or who earned as much as $1,000 per year. Now, along comes Mr.

Roosevelt and says that he is for the old-age pension of $30 a month, but he says that it shall be paid by the States. And he says up until January 1, 1940, this $30 a month may be paid by the States to those who are over 70 years of age and after that time to those who are 65 years of age. Then he says that before they can get the $30 a month that the State government has got to put up one-half of the $30, and then it shall be paid only to those who are needy. And then he says that in order to get the money for the part the Federal Government is going to put up, that they will put a tax on all payrolls, so that the money would be taken from the very source and class to whom it is intended it would be paid.

What the Roosevelt pronouncement for old-age pensions means is that he would scuttle it inside and out. In other words, he will proceed to show how unreasonable, how impossible an old-age pension system can be, and how much harm can be done by trying to bring it about. His plan contemplates that the Federal Government will contribute $125 million for old-age pensions throughout the United States. That is not a drop in the bucket. It will take $3 billion to pay an old-age pension to all people who are 60 years of age; and unless the United States Government puts up all of the $3 billion, you will not have any old age pension system that is worth anything.

Now, the only way you can get $3 billion is by taxing the billionaires and multimillionaires, and nobody else, because if you tax the poor wage earner, who is barely making a living now, you will do more harm than good in trying to build up an old-age pension system. All the worthy movements that have been advocated throughout the United States are always praised by Mr. Roosevelt, who prescribes, in order to carry them into effect, a remedy that means you try to pull yourself up by your own bootstraps.

He admits that most of the people of America are impoverished because the rich people have all the money. He says they ought not allow them to have it all, but in the next breath he gives out a statement that the big rich must not be taxed very much, and that is as far as we ever get with him. He rode into the President's office on the platform of redistributing wealth. He has done no such thing and has made no effort to do any such thing since he has been there.

There is only one relief that can come to the American people that is of any value whatever, and that is to redistribute wealth by limiting the size of the big men's fortunes and guaranteeing that, beginning at the bottom, every family will have a living and the comforts of life. We can pass laws today providing for education, for old-age pensions, for unemployment insurance, for doles, public buildings, and anything else that we could think of, and still none of them would be worth anything unless we provided the money for them.

And the money cannot be provided for them without these things doing twice as much harm as they do good unless that money is scraped off the big piles at the top and spread among the people at the bottom, who have nothing. Any man with a thimbleful of sense who would be trying to help the poor people today by taxing the poor people so as to give the money back to them, ought to be bored for the hollow horn. Now, Mr. Roosevelt has better sense than that, but he is faced with a proposition. He has made the promise to the people that he will tear down these big fortunes by putting some reasonable limit on them, and he has further promised to build up the little man from the bottom. But he feels he doesn't dare keep that promise; he doesn't dare to keep that promise, and so, what is he doing? He makes every kind of move showing he is for this and for that; that he wants to appropriate a little money--so much for this and so much for that--but when you wind up, you find what he actually does is, that if there is any tax that can be levied on the poor people to give these things back to the poor people, that then he prescribes that kind of cure that never has cured or will cure.

58

The big interests realize Roosevelt's plan would not cost them anything, which is the same as saying it will be no relief to the poor. Here is the proof of that admission from the financial page of the New York Times of January 18, 1935:

The action of the stock markets yesterday indicated that Wall Street was not alarmed by the President's message to Congress on social security legislation. The financial community had been hopeful that the plan would not be so ambitious as to retard recovery. By its freedom from liquidation, when the message appeared on the news tickers, the market indicated that Wall Street did not feel that the plan would increase taxation unduly, since it would be largely self-sustaining.

What Wall Street is saying by this dispatch is that the big men of Wall Street were a little bit apprehensive for fear Roosevelt would provide some relief or social legislation that would cost them something, but they are glad to see whatever he does will be self-sustaining. That is, the poor people who get relief will pay for it. In other words, the poor people will be allowed to help the poor people, a poor wage earner will be allowed to help his aged father or mother and take away a little more from his wife and children. "Ain't" that grand? Yet Wall Street says they are much pleased with it because it means they will not be touched for the necessary money to cure the ills of our people.

Now, our conditions today are much more deplorable than they were in [Herbert] Hoover's depression. The Roosevelt depression is just a double dose of the Hoover depression. In 1929 we started out with the public debt under Hoover of $16,931,000,000, and we wound up under Hoover with his depression showing a public debt of $19,487,000,000, or an increase of $2 billion practically all of which increase under Hoover, however, was covered by loans made by the Reconstruction Finance Corporation, for which it had adequate security and collateral, and so, in fact, there was scarcely any such thing as an increase in the public debt under Hoover as compared to Roosevelt.

So we started in, in 1933, with the Roosevelt depression, starting from the Hoover national debt figure of $19,487,000,000. Now, when we got to December 31, 1934, the national deficit had been raised by the Roosevelt depression to $28,478,000,000, or an increase of approximately $9 billion and most of it is just that much more debt, good and simple. Now, how much good has been done with it? Has it cured unemployment? Get ready to laugh, if crying will do it. I will give you some unemployment figures that will shed the light as it ought to be. Here they are as they exist today:

UNEMPLOYMENT FIGURES
Half the working people in America are unemployed today Industrial unemployment: American Federation of Labor--1934--November__ 10,659,000 Farm unemployment: Figure farm unemployment on the basis that 1929 was a normal year. That year the farm population was 30,257,000 and earned $11,941,000,000, or $394 to every farm person-- that much in Hoover's first depression year. In 1933 the farm population increased by 2 million to 32,509,000 persons who earned for the whole year $6,256,000,000 less $271,000,000 given by the Government, or the sum of $184 to the person, or 46 percent as much per farm person as under Hoover's first depression year. So the only thing that we can say is that the farm labor of 1933, as compared to the farm labor of 1929, was 54 percent unemployed so far as earnings go, and that is all that counts in unemployment figures. Figuring that 40 percent of the farm population does not work, that leaves us to figures that 19,620,000 persons are normally employed on the farm, and if we take 54 percent of them as unemployed, which they are on the basis of 1929 earnings compared to 1933 earnings, we add to the unemployed list farm laborers numbering _ _ _ _ 10,594,800 Making the unemployed total _ _ _ _ 21,253,000

60

Knowing that one employed person may be the breadwinner of anywhere from 1.5 to 5 persons, this figure of 21,253,000 unemployed persons presents a total unemployment picture of nearly half the American people. It is about equally balanced, one-half unemployed to industry and one-half to agriculture. This does not even include the professional man as unemployed. The lawyer, doctor, accountant, architect, dentist, grocer, baker, and candlestick maker, who cannot make a living because the people have nothing to spend with them, are not even listed as unemployed, though if the proper thing were done they would increase the list another 2,000,000 unemployed.

The figure of 10,659,000 unemployed in the industrial class would be materially increased if we included as a percentage of unemployment those working part time, some down to as low as 1 day per week. Note also that even those who are employed earn a wage which is 43 percent below a fair standard of living. (See American Federation of Labor bulletin of January 12, 1935.) So you see from the Government's own figures that the estimate of one-half of all our people as unemployed does not near tell the whole story. It would be very interesting if you would just take a look to see how well the people who are employed are getting along. I have here the monthly survey of business of the American Federation of Labor dated January 12, 1935. It says this: Comparing 1934 with 1933, according to the records, we have-- 1. Average yearly wage: The worker's average yearly wage has increased 6.7 percent in these industries, while the price of food rose 11.3 percent and prices of clothing and house furnishings rose 15.3 percent. Clearly, the average employed worker's standard of living was lower in 1934 than 1933, although his average yearly income rose from $1,029 to $1,099 in 1934. 2. The average worker's income of nearly $1,099 in 1934 is below the minimum necessary to support a family of five in health and decency by $813, or 43 percent. In other words, according to these accredited figures, those so fortunate as to be employed are living 43 percent below a reasonable standard of living at the end of the year 1934 under Roosevelt's depression.

So we sum up our condition:

We compare the Roosevelt depression with the Hoover depression and we find the Roosevelt depression debt is $9 billion more than the Hoover depression debt; the unemployment under Roosevelt has eclipsed everything Hoover ever heard about, and approximates mores than one-half the whole population of America; the wage earner of today is living further below the standard of a fair living than ever before in the history of the country; the wealth of the country is more in the hands of the big interests and the big men than it has ever been, and the common people and masses in general have less than they ever had; two-thirds of all of the money in the banks is owned by one-one hundred and fiftieth of the people, according to the figures furnished by the Government bureau itself; there are 5 million more people on the dole than there were last year, and another 5 million people trying to get on the dole. We have the same promises from Mr. Roosevelt now that we had before he was elected, with the exception he says you must not pass any such law as will put them into effect in actual fact.

The only difference in Roosevelt before election and now is that Roosevelt now says he is still for them, but that you must not do anything about them. The only difference between Mr. Roosevelt and Mr. Hoover is that things are much worse in every degree under Mr. Roosevelt than ever under Mr. Hoover; and you could tell what Mr. Hoover meant to do, or rather meant not to do, whereas understanding what Mr. Roosevelt means to do compared to what he does do is difficult.

There is only one way to save our people; only one way to save America. How? Pull down wealth from the top and spread wealth at the bottom; free people of these debts they owe; God told just exactly how to do it all. Many other countries have been in the shape that America is in now;

many fell and vanished like Rome and Greece, but some cared for their people and were saved.

There was once a country in exactly the same shape as America is today. God's prophet was there and applied the laws as God had prescribed them. If you would just recognize that God is still alive, that His law still lives, America would not grope today. Here is the written record of that country that was in the same fix as America is today.

Here is what they did under the command of God's prophet. Hear me, I read from the Bible, Nehemiah, chapter 5: And there was a great cry of the people and of their wives against their brethren the Jews. For there were that said, We, our sons, and our daughters, are many: therefore we take up corn for them, that we may eat, and live. Some also there were that said, We have mortgaged our lands, vineyards, and houses, that we might buy corn, because of the dearth. There were also that said, We have borrowed money for the king's tribute, and that upon our lands and vineyards. Yet now our flesh is as the flesh of our brethren, our children as their children; and, lo, we bring into bondage our sons and our daughters to be servants, and some of our daughters are brought into bondage already; neither is it in our power to redeem them; for other men have our lands and vineyards. And I was very angry when I heard their cry and these words. Then I consulted with myself, and I rebuked the nobles, and the rulers, and said unto them, Ye exact usury, every one of his brother. And I set a great assembly against them. And I said unto them, We after our ability have redeemed our brethren the Jews, which were sold unto the heathen, and will ye even sell your brethren? or shall they be sold unto us? Then held they their peace, and found nothing to answer. Also, I said, it is not good that ye do; ought ye not to walk in the fear of our God because of the reproach of the heathen our enemies? I likewise, and my brethren, and my servants, might exact of them money and corn; I pray you, let us leave off this usury. Restore, I pray you, to them, even this day, their lands, their vineyards, their olive yards, and their houses, also the hundredth part of the money, and of the corn, the wine, and the oil, that ye exact of them. Then said they, We will restore them, and will require nothing of them, so will we do as thou sayest. Then I called the priests, and took an oath of them, that they should do according to this promise. Also I shook my lap, and said, So God shake out every man from his house, and from his labor, that performeth not this promise, even thus be he shaken out, and emptied. And all the congregation said, Amen, and praised the Lord. And the people did according to this promise.

Hear me, people of America, God's laws live today. Keep them and none suffer, disregard them and we go the way of the missing. His word said that. Here is what He said: "The profit of the earth is for all." Ecclesiastes: chapter 5, verse 9. "And ye shall hallow the fiftieth year, and proclaim liberty throughout all the land unto all the inhabitants thereof; it shall be a jubilee unto you; and ye shall return every man unto his possession, and ye shall return every man unto his family."

Leviticus: chapter 25. verse 10.

"At the end of every 7 years thou shalt make a release. . . Every creditor that lendeth ought unto his neighbor shall release it; he shall not exact it of his. . . brother; because it is called the Lord's release." Deuteronomy: Chapter 15, verses 1 and 2.

Maybe you do not believe the Bible; maybe you do not accept God as your Supreme Lawgiver. God help you if you do not; but if you do not, then all I ask of you is to believe the simple problems of arithmetic, the tables of addition, subtraction, multiplication, and division. If you believe them, you will know that we cannot tolerate this condition of a handful of people owning nearly all and all owning nearly nothing. In a land of plenty there is no need to starve unless we allow greed to starve us to please the vanity of someone else. I can read you what Theodore Roosevelt, Daniel Webster, Thomas Jefferson, Abraham Lincoln, Ralph Waldo Emerson, all other great Americans said. Their beliefs might be stated in the following lines of Emerson: "Give no bounties: make equal laws: secure life and prosperity and you need not give alms." Or maybe these words of Theodore Roosevelt would be proof: "We must pay equal attention to the distribution of prosperity. The only prosperity worth having is that which affects the mass of people."

It was the poet Horace who warned that Rome would fall in the days of Augustus Caesar. He expressed the line: "Penniless and great plenty." So are our American people today. Too much to eat, to wear, or to live in; too much, and yet we are penniless and starve.

Here are the words of Pope Pius in his encyclical letter of May 18,1932, which I, a Baptist, caused to be placed in the CONGRESSIONAL RECORD. Hear these words:

From greed arises mutual distrust that casts a blight on all human dealings; from greed arises hateful envy which makes a man consider the advantages of another as losses to himself; from greed arises narrow individualism which orders and subordinates everything to its own advantage without taking account of others, on the contrary, cruelly trampling under foot all rights of others. Hence the disorder and inequality from which arises the accumulation of the wealth of nations in the hands of a small group of individuals who manipulate the market of the world at their own caprice, to the immense harm of the masses, as we showed last year in our encyclical letter.

I call and ask you now to organize a share-our-wealth society in your community now. Don't delay. If you want to know more about it, write to me in Washington. If you want a copy of this speech, write to me for it. Help in our plan. What is it? I state it to you again: We propose to limit the size of all big fortunes to not more than $3 to 4 million and to throw the balance in the United States Treasury; we will impose taxes every year to keep down these fortunes and to also limit the amount which any one may earn to $1 million per year, and to limit the amount any one can inherit to $1 million in a lifetime, throwing all surpluses into the United States Treasury.

Then from the immense money thus acquired we will guarantee to every family a home and the comforts of a home, including such conveniences as automobile and radio; we will guarantee education to every child and youth through college and vocational training, based upon the ability of the student and not upon the ability of the child's parents to pay the costs; we would pay flat and outright to all people over 60 years of age, a pension sufficient for their life and comfort; we would shorten the hours of work to 30 hours per week, maybe less, and to eleven months per year, maybe less; and thus share our work at living wages and to those for whom we fail to find work we would pay insurance until we do find it; we would pay the soldiers' bonus and give a sufficient supply of money to carry on our work and business. All this can be done with ease only if we will say to the rich, "None shall be too rich!"

Won't you help in this work? Is not humanity worth the effort? How much do we need it? I will tell you. Hear me now read you a report from our newspapers. It reads: BABE DYING, MOTHER WALKS STREET IN HUNT FOR AID--BRAVES BITTER COLD WHEN CHILD GROWS WORSE; FINDS NO RELIEF AT WELFARE STATION, IS TOLD TO GO TO HOSPITAL, WALKS IN VAIN

By United Press CHICAGO, January 16.--It was bitterly cold. Frail Mrs. Ella Martindale huddled with her four children close to an insufficient stove. The baby, 5 months old, wailed fitfully in fever under blankets on the floor. All awaited return of Murrian Martindale, the father, who promised when he left for his shift as a cab driver that "I'll bring something to eat, some way."The baby's cries grew more frequent but weaker. She refused the warm water offered as a substitute for milk. Paroxysms purpled her tiny face and the older children, from 3 to 12, whimpered in sympathy and fear. Mrs. Martindale paced the floor, wrung her hands. A strangling cough wracked the infant girl. The mother acted in desperation. Whirling blankets around the baby and a ragged coat around her own shoulders, she ordered the oldest girl to watch the other children. She raced from the room, carrying the sick child. At an infant welfare station two blocks away she sobbed out her troubles. The women on duty were sorry, but no doctor would be present for hours. They advised her to go to St. Joseph's Hospital. Mrs. Martindale had no car fare but she went. She walked-- six blocks--with the thermometer at 16 above zero. She stumbled on the steps into the hospital.My baby," she sobbed to a nurse, "she's sick." The nurse peered into the blankets, then took the little bundle."She's dead," she said.

Good night, my friends. I thank you!

An excerpt from another class war speech by Sen Long:

We owe debts in America today, public and private, amounting to $252 billion. That means that every child is born with a $2,000 debt tied around his neck to hold him down before he gets started. Then, on top of that, the wealth is locked in a vice owned by a few people. We propose that children shall be born in a land of opportunity, guaranteed a home, food, clothes, and the other things that make for living, including the right to education.

Our plan would injure no one. It would not stop us from having millionaires--it would increase them tenfold, because so many more people could make a million dollars if they had the chance our plan gives them. Our plan would not break up big concerns. The only difference would be that maybe 10,000 people would own a concern instead of 10 people owning it. But my friends, unless we do share our wealth, unless we limit the size of the big man so as to give something to the little man, we can never have a happy or free people. God said so! He ordered it.

We have everything our people need. Too much of food, clothes, and houses why not let all have their fill and lie down in the ease and comfort God has given us? Why not? Because a few own everything--the masses own nothing. I wonder if any of you people who are listening to me were ever at a barbecue! We used to go there--sometimes a thousand people or more. If there were 1,000 people we would put enough meat and bread and everything else on the table for 1,000 people. Then everybody would be called and everyone would eat all they wanted. But suppose at one of these barbecues for 1,000 people that one man took 90 percent of the food and ran off with t and ate until he got sick and let the balance rot. Then 999 people would have only enough for 100 to eat and there would be many to starve because of the greed of just one person for something he couldn't eat himself.

Well, ladies and gentlemen, America, all the people of America, have been invited to a barbecue. God invited us all to come and eat and drink all we wanted. He smiled on our land and we grew crops of plenty to eat and wear. He showed us in the earth the iron and other things to make everything we wanted. He unfolded to us the secrets of science so that our work might be easy. God called: "Come to my feast." Then what happened? Rockefeller, Morgan, and their crowd stepped up and took enough for 120 million people and left only enough for 5 million for all the other 125 million to eat. And so many millions must go hungry and without these good things God gave us unless we call on them to put some of it back.I call on you to organize share-our-wealth societies. Write to me in Washington if you will help.

Let us dry the eyes of those who suffer; let us lift the hearts of the sad. There is plenty. There is more. Why should we not secure laws to do justice--laws that were promised to

us--never should we have quibbled over the soldiers' bonus.
We need that money circulating among our people. That is
why I offered the amendment to pay it last year. I will do so
again this year

Why weep or slumber, America?
Land of brave and true,
With castles, clothing, and food for all
All belongs to you.
Ev'ry man a king, ev'ry man a king,
For you can be a millionaire;
But there's something belonging to others,
There's enough for all people to share.
When it's sunny June and December, too,
Or in the wintertime or spring,
There'll be peace without end,
Ev'ry neighbor a friend,
With ev'ry man a king.
United States Senate,
Washington, D. C.

All material from the Congressional Record.

Adolf Hitler

What follows is one of the speeches that made Adolph Hitler famous. He was on trial for treason, he decided in a brilliant move to use the trial to attack the tribunal and the state, rather than defend his actions. We see here the use of emotional appeals, and of scapegoating, the offering of Jews as the real reason for Germany's problems, served up by history's most evil genius who we hope is in the hottest region of hell.

BEFORE THE MUNICH COURT

SPEECH OF FEBRUARY 26, 1924

IT SEEMS strange to me that a man who, as a soldier, was for six years accustomed to blind obedience, should suddenly come into conflict with the State and its Constitution. The reasons for this stem from the days of my youth. When I was seventeen I came to Vienna, and there I learned to study and observe three important problems: the social question, the race problem, and, finally, the Marxist movement. I left Vienna a confirmed anti-Semite, a deadly foe of the whole Marxist world outlook, and pan-German in my political principles. And since I knew that the German destiny of German-Austria would not be fought out in the Austrian Army alone, but in the German and Austrian Army, I enlisted in the German Army....

When, on November 7, [1918] it was announced that the Revolution had broken out in Munich, I at first could not believe it. At that time there arose in me the determination to devote myself to politics. I went through the period of the Soviets, and as a result of my opposition to them I came in contact with the National Socialist German Workers Movement, which at that time numbered six members. I was the seventh. I attached myself to this party, and not to one of the great political parties where my prospects would have been better, because none of the other parties understood or even recognized the decisive, fundamental problem.

By Marxism I understand a doctrine which in principle rejects the idea of the worth of personality, which replaces individual energy by the masses and thereby works the destruction of our whole cultural life. This movement has utilized monstrously effective methods and exercised tremendous influence on the masses, which in the course of three or four decades could have no other result than that the individual has become his own brother's foe, while at the same time calling a Frenchman, an Englishman, or a Zulu his brother. This movement is distinguished by incredible terror, which is based on a knowledge of mass psychology....

The German Revolution is a revolution, and therefore successful high treason; it is well known that such treason is never punished....

For us it was a filthy crime against the German people, a stab in the back of the German nation. The middle class could not take up arms against it because the middle class did not understand the whole revolution. It was necessary to start a new struggle and to incite against the Marxist despoilers of the people who did not even belong to the German race - which is where the Marxist problem is linked with the race problem, forming one of the most difficult and profound questions of our time....

Personally, at the beginning I held a lost position. Nevertheless, in the course of a few years there has grown from a little band of six men a movement which today embraces millions and which, above all, has once made the broad masses nationalistic....

In 1923 came the great and bitter scandal. As early as 1922 we had seen that the Ruhr was about to be lost. France's aim was not merely to weaken Germany, to keep her from obtaining supremacy, but to break her up into small states so that she [France] would be able to hold the Rhine frontier. After all the Government's reiterations of our weakness, we knew that on top of the Saar and Upper Silesia we would lose our third coal region, the Ruhr; each loss brought on the next one....

Only burning, ruthless, brutal fanaticism could have saved the situation. The Reich Government should have let the hundreds of thousands of young men who were pouring out of the Ruhr into the Reich under the old colors of black-white-red flow together in a mighty national wave. Instead, these young people were sent back home. The resistance that was organized was for wages; the national resistance was degraded to a paid general strike. It was forgotten that a foe like France cannot be prayed away, still less can he be idled away....

Our youth has - and may this be heard in Paris - but one thought: that the day may come when we shall again be free. .. .. My attitude is this: I would rather that Germany go Bolshevist and I be hanged than that she should be destroyed by the French rule of the sword.... It turned out that the back-stabbers were stronger than ever.... With pride I admit that our men were the only ones to really resist in the Ruhr. We intended to hold fourteen meetings and introduce a propaganda campaign throughout Germany with the slogan: DOWN WITH THE RUHR TRAITORS!, But we were surprised by the banning of these mass meetings. I had met Herr von Kahr in 1920. Kahr had impressed me as being an honest official. I asked him why the fourteen mass meetings had been banned. The reason he gave me simply would not hold water. THE REAL REASON WAS SOMETHING THAT COULD NOT BE REVEALED. . - -

From the very first day the watchword was: UNLIMITED STRUGGLE AGAINST BERLIN....

The struggle against Berlin, as Dr. von Kahr would lead it, is a crime; one must have the courage to be logical and see that the struggle must be incorporated in the German national uprising. I said that all that had been made of this struggle was a Bavarian rejection of Berlin's requests. But the people expected something other than a reduction in the price of beer, regulation of the price of milk and confiscation of butter tubs and other such impossible economic proposals - proposals which make you want to ask: who is the genius that is advising them? Every failure could only further enrage the masses, and I pointed out that while the people were now only laughing at Kahr's measures, later on they would rise up against them. I said: 'Either you finish the job - and there is only the political and military struggle left. When you cross the Rubicon, you must march on Rome. Or else you do not want to struggle; then only capitulation is left....'

The struggle had to turn toward the North; it could not be led by a purely Bavarian organization . . . I said: 'The only man to head it is Ludendorff.'

I had first seen Ludendorff in 1918, in the field. In 1920 I first spoke personally with him. I saw that he was not only the outstanding general, but that he had now learned the lesson and understood what had brought the German nation to ruin. That Ludendorff was talked down by the others was one more reason

73

for me to come closer to him. I therefore proposed Ludendorff, and Lossow and Seisser had no objections.

I further explained to Lossow that right now nothing could be accomplished by petty economic measures. The fight was against Marxism. To solve this problem, not administrators were needed but firebrands who would be in a position to inflame the national spirit to the extreme. Kahr could not do that, I pointed out; the youth were not behind him. I declared that I could join them only on the condition that the political struggle was put into my hands alone. This was not impudence or immodesty; I believe that when a man knows he can do a job, he must not be modest....

One thing was certain: Lossow, Kahr, and Seisser had the same goal that we had: to get rid of the Reich Government with its present international and parliamentary position, and to replace it by an anti-parliamentary government. If our undertaking was actually high treason, then during this whole period Lossow, Seisser, and Kahr must have been committing high treason along with us - for during all those months we talked of nothing but the aims of which we now stand accused....

How could we have called for a new government if we had not known that the gentlemen in power were altogether on our side? How else could we, two days before, have given such orders as: at 8:30 o'clock such and such a government will be proclaimed....

Lossow talked of a coup d'etat. Kahr quite openly declared that he would give the word to strike. The only possible interpretation of this talk is that these men wanted to strike, but each time lost their nerve. Our last conversation, on November 6, was for me the

absolute confirmation of my belief that these men wanted to, but -
!....

BEFORE THE MUNICH COURT

SPEECH OF MARCH 27, 1924

WHEN did the ruin of Germany begin? You know
the watchword of the old German system in its
foreign policy: it ran - maintenance of world peace,
economic conquest of the world. With both these
principles one cannot govern a people. The
maintenance of world peace cannot be the purpose
and aim of the policy of a State. The increase and
maintenance of a people - that alone can be the aim. If
you are going to conquer the world by an economic
policy, other peoples will not fail to see their danger.

What is the State? Today the State is an economic
organization, an association of persons, formed, it
would seem, for the sole purpose that all should co
operate in securing each other's daily bread. THE
STATE, HOWEVER, IS NOT AN ECONOMIC
ORGANIZATION, IT IS A 'VOLKIC' ORGANISM.
The purpose, the aim of the State is to provide the
people with its food-supply and with the position of
power in the world which is its due. Germany
occupies in Europe perhaps the most bitter situation
of any people, Militarily, politically, and
geographically it is surrounded by none but rivals: IT
CAN MAINTAIN ITSELF ONLY WHEN IT
PLACES A POWER-POLICY (MACHTPOLITIK)
RUTHLESSLY IN THE FOREGROUND.

Two Powers are in a position to determine the future
development of Europe: England and France.

England's aim remains eternally the same: to balkanize Europe and to establish a balance of power in Europe so that her position in the world will not be threatened. ENGLAND IS NOT ON PRINCIPLE AN ENEMY OF GERMANY, IT IS THE POWER WHICH SEEKS TO GAIN THE FIRST PLACE IN EUROPE. The declared enemy of Germany is France. Just as England needs the balkanization of Europe, so France needs the balkanization of Germany in order to gain hegemony in Europe. After four and a half years of bitter struggle at last through the Revolution the scale of victory turned in favor of the coalition of these two Powers, with the following result: France was faced with the question: Was she to realize her eternal war-aim or not? That means: Could France destroy Germany and deprive it of all the sources whereby its people was fed? Today France watches the ripening to fulfillment of her age-old plan: it matters not what Government will be at the helm in France: the supreme aim will remain - the annihilation of Germany, the extermination of twenty million Germans, and the dissolution of Germany into separate States....

The army which we have formed grows from day to day; from hour to hour it grows more rapidly. EVEN NOW I HAVE THE PROUD HOPE THAT ONE DAY THE HOUR IS COMING WHEN THESE UNTRAINED BANDS WILL BECOME BATTALIONS, WHEN THE BATTALIONS WILL BECOME REGIMENTS AND THE REGIMENTS DIVISIONS, when the old cockade will be raised from the mire, when the old banners will once again wave before us: and then reconciliation will come in that eternal last Court of Judgment - the Court of God - before which we are ready to take our stand. Then from our bones, from our graves will sound the voice of that tribunal which alone has the right to sit in judgment upon us. For, gentlemen, it is not you who pronounce judgment upon us, it is the eternal Court of History which will make its pronouncement upon the charge which is brought against us. The judgment that you will pass, that I know. But that Court will not ask of us: 'Have you committed high treason or not?' That Court will judge us ....who as Germans have wished the best for their people and their Fatherland, who wished to fight and to die. You may declare us guilty a thousand times, but the Goddess who presides over the Eternal Court of History will with a smile tear in pieces the charge of the Public Prosecutor and the judgment of the Court: for she declares us guiltless.

Adolf Hitler blaming a world Jewish Conspiracy, just before he seals his doom with the invasion of Russia:

BERLIN, REICHSTAG

SPEECH OF MAY 4, 1941

Deputies. Men of the German Reichstag:

At a time when only deeds count and words are of little importance, it is not my intention to appear before you, the elected representatives of the German people, more often than absolutely necessary. The first time I spoke to you was at the outbreak of the war when, thanks to the Anglo-French conspiracy against peace, every attempt at an understanding with Poland, which otherwise would have been possible, had been frustrated.

The most unscrupulous men of the present time had, as they admit today, decided as early as 1936 to involve the Reich, which in its peaceful work of reconstruction was becoming too powerful for them, in a new and bloody war and, if possible, to destroy it. They had finally succeeded in finding a State that was prepared for their interests and aims, and that State was Poland.

All my endeavors to come to an understanding with Britain were wrecked by the determination of a small clique which, whether from motives of hate or for the sake of material gain, rejected every German proposal for an understanding due to their resolve, which they never concealed, to resort to war, whatever happened.

The man behind this fanatical and diabolical plan to bring about war at whatever cost was Mr. Churchill.

His associates were the men who now form the British Government.

These endeavors received most powerful support, both openly and secretly, from the so-called great democracies on both sides of the Atlantic. At a time when the people were more and more dissatisfied with their deficient statesmanship, the responsible men over there believed that a successful war would be the most likely means of solving problems that otherwise would be beyond their power to solve.

Behind these men there stood the great international Jewish financial interests that control the banks and the Stock Exchange as well as the armament industry. And now, just as before, they scented the opportunity of doing their unsavory business. And so, just as before, there was no scruple about sacrificing the blood of the peoples. That was the beginning of this war. A few weeks later the State that was the third country in Europe, Poland, but had been reckless enough to allow herself to be used for the financial interests of these warmongers, was annihilated and destroyed.

In these circumstances I considered that I owed it to our German people and countless men and women in the opposite camps, who as individuals were as decent as they were innocent of blame, to make yet another appeal to the common sense and the conscience of these statesmen. On October 6, 1939, I therefore once more publicly stated that Germany had neither demanded nor intended to demand anything either from Britain or from France, that it was madness to continue the war and, above all, that the scourge of modern weapons of warfare, once they were brought into action, would inevitably ravage vast territories.

But just as the appeal I made on September 1, 1939, proved to be in vain, this renewed appeal met with indignant rejection. The British and their Jewish capitalist backers could find no other explanation for this appeal, which I had made on humanitarian grounds, than the assumption of weakness on the part of Germany.

They assured the people of Britain and France that Germany dreaded the clash to be expected in the spring of 1940 and was eager to make peace for fear of the annihilation that would then inevitably result.

Already at that time the Norwegian Government, misled by the stubborn insistence of Mr. Churchill's false prophecies, began to toy with the idea of a British landing on their soil, thereby contributing to the destruction of Germany by permitting their harbors and Swedish iron ore fields to be seized.

So sure were Mr. Churchill and Paul Reynaud of the success of their new scheme that finally, whether from sheer recklessness or perhaps under the influence of drink, they deemed it no longer necessary to make a secret of their intentions.

It was thanks to these two gentlemen's tendency to gossip that the German Government at that time gained cognizance of the plans being made against the Reich. A few weeks later this danger to Germany was eliminated. One of the boldest deeds of arms in the whole history of warfare frustrated the attack of the British and French armies against the right flank of our line of defense.

Immediately after the failure of these plans, increased pressure was exerted by the British warmongers upon Belgium and Holland. Now that the attack upon our sources for the supply of iron ore had proved unsuccessful, they aimed to advance the front to the Rhine by involving the Belgian and Dutch States and thus to threaten and paralyze our production centers for iron and steel.

On May 10 of last year perhaps the most memorable struggle in all German history commenced. The enemy front was broken up in a few days and the stage was then set for the operation that culminated in the greatest battle of annihilation in the history of the world. Thus France collapsed, Belgium and Holland were already occupied, and the battered remnants of the British expeditionary force were driven from the European continent, leaving their arms behind.

On July 19, 1940, I then convened the German Reichstag for the third time in order to render that great account which you all still remember. The meeting provided me with the opportunity of expressing the thanks of the nation to its soldiers in a form suited to the uniqueness of the event. Once again I seized the opportunity of urging the world to make peace. And what I foresaw and prophesied at that time happened. My offer of peace was misconstrued as a symptom of fear and cowardice.

The European and American warmongers succeeded once again in befogging the sound common sense of the masses, who can never hope to profit from this war, by conjuring up false pictures of new hope. Thus, finally, under pressure of public opinion, as formed by their press, they once more managed to induce the nation to continue this struggle.

Even my warnings against night bombings of the civilian population, as advocated by Mr. Churchill, were interpreted as a sign of German impotence. He, the most bloodthirsty or amateurish strategist that history has ever known, actually saw fit to believe

81

that the reserve displayed for months by the German Air Force could be looked upon only as proof of their incapacity to fly by night.

So this man for months ordered his paid scribblers to deceive the British people into believing that the Royal Air Force alone - and no others - was in a position to wage war in this way, and that thus ways and means had been found to force the Reich to its knees by the ruthless onslaught of the British Air Force on the German civilian population in conjunction with the starvation blockade.

Again and again I uttered these warnings against this specific type of aerial warfare, and I did so for over three and a half months. That these warnings failed to impress Mr. Churchill does not surprise me in the least. For what does this man care for the lives of others? What does he care for culture or for architecture? When war broke out he stated clearly that he wanted to have his war, even though the cities of England might be reduced to ruins. So now he has got his war.

My assurances that from a given moment every one of his bombs would be returned if necessary a hundredfold failed to induce this man to consider even for an instant the criminal nature of his action. He professes not to be in the least depressed and he even assures us that the British people, too, after such bombing raids, greeted him with a joyous serenity, causing him to return to London refreshed by his visits to the stricken areas.

It is possible that this sight strengthened Mr. Churchill in his firm determination to continue the war in this way, and we are no less determined to continue to retaliate, if necessary, a hundred bombs for every one of his and to go on doing so until the

British nation at last gets rid of this criminal and his methods.

The appeal to forsake me, made to the German nation by this fool and his satellites on May Day, of all days, are only to be explained either as symptomatic of a paralytic disease or of a drunkard's ravings. His abnormal state of mind also gave birth to a decision to transform the Balkans into a theater of war.

For over five years this man has been chasing around Europe like a madman in search of something that he could set on fire. Unfortunately, he again and again finds hirelings who open the gates of their country to this international incendiary.

After he had succeeded in the course of the past winter in persuading the British people by a wave of false assertions and pretensions that the German Reich, exhausted by the campaign in the preceding months, was completely spent, he saw himself obliged, in order to prevent an awakening of the truth, to create a fresh conflagration in Europe.

In so doing he returned to the project that had been in his mind as early as the autumn of 1939 and the spring of 1940. It was thought possible at the time to mobilize about 100 divisions in Britain's interest.

The sudden collapse which we witnessed in May and June of the past year forced these plans to be abandoned for the moment. But by the autumn of last year Mr. Churchill began to tackle this problem once again.

In the meantime, however, certain difficulties had arisen. As a result, Rumania, owing to internal changes, dropped out of England's political scheme.

In dealing with these conditions, I shall begin by giving you a brief outline of the aims of Germany's policy in the Balkans. As in the past, the Reich never pursued any territorial or any other selfish political interest in the Balkans. In other words, the Reich has never taken the slightest interest in territorial problems and internal conditions in these States for any selfish reason whatsoever.

On the other hand, the Reich has always endeavored to build up and to strengthen close economic ties with these States in particular. This, however, not only served the interests of the Reich but equally the interests of these countries themselves.

If any two national economic systems ever effectively complemented one another, that is especially the case regarding the Balkan States and Germany. Germany is an industrial country and requires foodstuffs and raw materials. The Balkan States are agrarian countries and are short of these raw materials. At the same time, they require industrial products.

It was therefore hardly surprising when Germany thus became the main business partner of the Balkan States. Nor was this in Germany's interest alone, but also in that of the Balkan peoples themselves.

AND NONE BUT OUR JEW-RIDDEN DEMOCRACIES, WHICH CAN THINK ONLY IN TERMS OF CAPITALISM, CAN MAINTAIN THAT IF ONE STATE DELIVERS MACHINERY TO ANOTHER STATE IT THEREBY DOMINATES THAT OTHER STATE. IN ACTUAL FACT SUCH DOMINATION, IF IT OCCURS, CAN BE ONLY A RECIPROCAL DOMINATION.

It is presumably easier to be without machinery than without food and raw materials. Consequently, the

84

partner in need of raw material and foodstuffs would appear to be more tied down than the recipient of industrial products. IN THIS TRANSACTION THERE WAS NEITHER CONQUEROR NOR CONQUERED. THERE WERE ONLY PARTNERS.

The German Reich of the National Socialist revolution has prided itself on being a fair and decent partner, offering in exchange high-quality products instead of worthless democratic paper money. For these reasons the Reich was interested in only one thing if, indeed, there was any question of political interest, namely, in seeing that internally the business partner was firmly established on a sound and healthy basis.

THE APPLICATION OF THIS IDEA LED IN FACT NOT ONLY TO INCREASING PROSPERITY IN THESE COUNTRIES BUT ALSO TO THE BEGINNING OF MUTUAL CONFIDENCE. All the greater, however, became the endeavor of that world incendiary, Churchill, to put an end to this peaceful development and by shamelessly imposing upon these States utterly worthless British guarantees and promises of assistance to introduce into this peaceable European territory elements of unrest, uncertainty, distrust and, finally, conflict.

Originally, Rumania was first won over by these guarantees and later, of course, Greece. It has, meanwhile, probably been sufficiently demonstrated that he had absolutely no power of any kind to provide real help and that these guarantees were merely intended to rope these States in to follow the dangerous trend of filthy British politics.

RUMANIA HAS HAD TO PAY BITTERLY FOR THE GUARANTEES, WHICH WERE

CALCULATED TO ESTRANGE HER FROM THE
AXIS POWERS.

Greece, which least of all required such a guarantee,
was offered her share to link her destiny to that of the
country that provided her King with cash and orders.

EVEN TODAY I FEEL THAT I MUST, AS I
BELIEVE IN THE INTEREST OF HISTORICAL
ACCURACY, DISTINGUISH BETWEEN THE
GREEK PEOPLE AND THAT THIN TOP LAYER
OF CORRUPT LEADERS WHO, INSPIRED BY A
KING WHO HAD NO EYES FOR THE DUTY OF
TRUE LEADERSHIP, PREFERRED INSTEAD TO
FURTHER THE AIMS OF BRITISH WAR
POLITICS. To me this is a subject of profound regret.

Germany, with the faint hope of still being able to
contribute in some way to a solution of the problem,
had not severed relations with Greece. But even then I
was bound in duty to point out before the whole
world that we would not tacitly allow a revival of the
old Salonika scheme of the Great War.

Unfortunately, my warning was not taken seriously
enough. That we were determined, if the British tried
to gain another foothold in Europe, to drive them
back into the sea was not taken seriously enough.

The result was that the British began in an increasing
degree to establish bases for the formation of a new
Salonika army. They began by laying out airdromes
and by establishing the necessary ground organization
in the firm conviction that the occupation of the
airdromes themselves could afterward be carried out
very speedily.

Finally a continuous stream of transports brought
equipment for an army which, according to Mr.

Churchill's idea and plans, was to be landed in Greece. As I have said, already we were aware of this. For months we watched this entire strange procedure with attention, if with restraint.

The reverses suffered by the Italian Army in North Africa, owing to a certain material inferiority of their tanks and anti-tank guns, finally led Mr. Churchill to believe that the time was ripe to transfer the theater of war from Libya to Greece. He ordered the transport of the remaining tanks and of the infantry division, composed mainly of Anzacs, and was convinced that he could now complete his scheme, which was to set the Balkans aflame.

THUS DID MR. CHURCHILL COMMIT ONE OF THE GREATEST STRATEGIC BLUNDERS OF THIS WAR. As soon as there could be no further doubt regarding Britain's intentions of gaining a foothold in the Balkans, I took the necessary steps.

Germany, by keeping pace with these moves, assembled the necessary forces for the purpose of counteracting any possible tricks of that gentleman. In this connection I must state categorically that this action was not directed against Greece.

The Duce did not even request me to place one single German division at his disposal for this purpose. He was convinced that with the advent of good weather his stand against Greece would have been brought to a successful conclusion. I was of the same opinion.

The concentration of German forces was therefore not made for the purpose of assisting the Italians against Greece. It was a precautionary measure against the British attempt under cover of the clamor caused by the Italo-Greek war to intrench themselves secretly in the Balkans in order to force the issue from that quarter on the model of the Salonika army during the World War, and, above all, to draw other elements into the whirlpool.

This hope was founded principally on two States, namely, Turkey and Yugoslavia. But with these very States I have striven during the years since I came into power to establish close co-operation.

The World War actually started from Belgrade. Nevertheless, the German people, who are by nature so ready to forgive and forget, felt no animosity toward that country. Turkey was our ally in the World War. The unfortunate outcome of that struggle weighed upon that country just as heavily as it did upon us.

The great genius who created the new Turkey was the first to set a wonderful example of recovery to our allies whom fortune had at that time deserted and whom fate had dealt so terrible a blow. Whereas Turkey, thanks to the practical attitude of her leaders, preserved her independence in carrying out her own resolutions, Yugolsavia fell a victim to British intrigue.

Most of you, especially my old Party comrades among you, know what efforts I have made to establish a straightforward understanding and indeed friendly relations between Germany and Yugoslavia. In pursuance of this aim Herr von Ribbentrop, our Minister of Foreign Affairs, submitted to the Yugoslav Government proposals that were so outstanding and so fair that at least even the Yugoslav State of that time seemed to become increasingly eager for such close co-operation.

Germany had no intention of starting a war in the Balkans. On the contrary, it was our honest intention as far as possible to contribute to a settlement of the conflict with Greece by means that would be tolerable to the legitimate wishes of Italy.

The Duce not only consented to but lent his full support to our efforts to bring Yugoslavia into a close community of interests with our peace aims. Thus it finally became possible to induce the Yugoslav Government to join the Threepower Pact, which made no demands whatever on Yugoslavia but only offered that country advantages.

Thus on March 26 of this year a pact was signed in Vienna that offered the Yugoslav State the greatest future conceivable and could have assured peace for the Balkans. Believe me, gentlemen, on that day I left the beautiful city of the Danube truly happy not only because it seemed as though almost eight years of foreign policies had received their reward but also because I believed that perhaps at the last moment German intervention in the Balkans might not be necessary.

We were all stunned by the news of that coup, carried through by a handful of bribed conspirators who had brought about the event that caused the British Prime Minister to declare in joyous words that at last he had something good to report.

YOU WILL SURELY UNDERSTAND, GENTLEMEN, THAT WHEN I HEARD THIS I AT ONCE GAVE ORDERS TO ATTACK YUGOSLAVIA. To treat the, German Reich in this way is impossible. One cannot spent years in concluding a treaty that is in the interest of the other party merely to discover that this treaty has not only been broken overnight but also that it has been answered by the insulting of the representative of the German Reich, by the threatening of his military attache, by the injuring of the aide de camp of this attache, by the maltreating of numerous other Germans, by demolishing property, by laying waste the homes of German citizens and by terrorizing.

GOD KNOWS THAT I WANTED PEACE. But I can do nothing but protect the interests of the Reich with those means which, thank God, are at our disposal. I made my decision at that moment all the more calmly because I knew that I was in accord with Bulgaria, who had always remained unshaken in her loyalty to the German Reich, and with the equally justified indignation of Hungary.

Both of our old allies in the World War were bound to regard this action as a provocation emanating from the State that once before had set the whole of Europe on fire and had been guilty of the indescribable sufferings that befell Germany, Hungary, and Bulgaria in consequence.

The general directions of operations issued by me through the Supreme Command of the German forces on March 27 confronted the Army and the Air Force with a formidable task. By a mere turn of the hand an additional campaign had to be prepared. Units that had already arrived had to be moved about. Supplies of armaments had to be assured and the air force had to take over numerous improvised airports part of which were still under water.

WITHOUT THE SYMPATHETIC ASSISTANCE OF HUNGARY AND THE EXTREMELY LOYAL ATTITUDE OF RUMANIA IT WOULD HAVE BEEN VERY DIFFICULT TO CARRY OUT MY ORDERS IN THE SHORT TIME ENVISAGED.

I fixed April 6 as the day on which the attack was to begin. The main plan of operation was: First, to proceed with an army coming from Bulgaria against Thrace in Greece in the direction of the Aegean Sea.

The main striking strength of this army lay in its right wing, which was to force a passage through to Salonika by using mountain divisions and a division of tanks; second, to thrust forward with a second army with the object of establishing connection as speedily as possible with the Italian forces advancing from Albania. These two operations were to begin on April 6.

Third, a further operation, beginning on the eighth, provided for the break-through of an army from Bulgaria with the object of reaching the neighborhood of Belgrade. In conjunction with this, a German army corps was to occupy the Banat on the tenth.

In connection with these operations general agreement had been made with our allies, Italy and Hungary. Agreements as to co-operation had also been reached between the two air forces. The command of the German Armies operating against Macedonia and Greece was placed in the hands of Field Marshal von List, who had already particularly distinguished himself in the previous campaigns. Once more and under the most exacting conditions he carried out the task confronting him in truly superior fashion.

The forces advancing against Yugoslavia from the southwest and from Hungary were commanded by Col. Gen. von Weick. He, too, in a very short time with the forces under his command reached his objective.

The Army and SS detachments operating under Field Marshal von Brauchitsch, as Commander in Chief, and the Chief of the General Staff, Col. Gen. Halder, forced the Greek Army in Thrace to capitulate after only five days, established contact with the Italian forces advancing from Albania, occupied Salonika, and thus generally prepared the way for the difficult and glorious break-through via Larissa to Athens.

These operations were crowned by the occupation of the Peloponnesus and numerous Greek islands. A detailed appreciation of the achievements will be given by the German High Command.

The Air Force under the personal command of Reich Marshal Goering was divided into two main groups, commanded by Col. Gen. Loehr and General von Richthofen. It was their task, first, to shatter the enemy air force and to smash its ground organization; second, to attack every important military objective in the conspirators' headquarters at Belgrade, thus eliminating it from the very outset; third, by every manner of active co-operation everywhere with the fighting German troops to break the enemy's resistance, to impede the enemy's flight, to prevent as far as possible his embarkation.

The German armed forces have truly surpassed themselves in this campaign. There is only one way of characterizing that campaign:

Nothing is impossible for the German soldier. Historical justice, however, obliges me to say that of the opponents that have taken up arms against us, MOST PARTICULARLY THE GREEK SOLDIERS, HAVE FOUGHT WITH THE GREATEST BRAVERY AND CONTEMPT OF DEATH. They only capitulated when further resistance became impossible and therefore useless.

But I am now compelled to speak of the enemy who is the main cause of this conflict. As a German and as a soldier I consider it unworthy ever to revile a fallen enemy. But it seems to me to be necessary to defend the truth from the wild exaggerations of a man who as a soldier is a bad politician and as a politician is an equally bad soldier.

Mr. Churchill, who started this struggle, is endeavoring, as with regard to Norway or Dunkerque, to say something that sooner or later might perhaps he twisted around to resemble success. I do not consider that honorable but in his case it is understandable.

The gift Mr. Churchill possesses is the gift to lie with a pious expression on his face and to distort the truth until finally glorious victories are made out of the most terrible defeats.

A British Army of 60,000 to 70,000 men landed in Greece. Before the catastrophe the same man maintained, moreover, that it consisted of 240,000 men. The object of this army was to attack Germany from the south, inflict a defeat upon her, and from this point as in 1918 turn the tide of the war.

I prophesied more correctly than Mr. Churchill in my last speech, in which I announced that wherever the British might set foot on the Continent they would be attacked by us and driven into the sea.

Now, with his brazen effrontery, he asserts that this war has cost us 75,000 lives. He causes his presumably not overintelligent fellow-countrymen to be informed by one of his paid creatures that the British, after having slain enormous masses of Germans, finally turned away from sheer abhorrence of the slaughter and, strictly speaking, withdrew for this reason alone.

I will now present to you the results of this campaign in a few short figures. In the course of the operations against Yugoslavia there were the following numbers of purely Serbian prisoners, leaving out soldiers of German origin and some other groups, 6,198 officers, 313,864 men.

The number of Greek prisoners, 8,000 officers and 210,000 men, has not the same significance. The number of Englishmen, New Zealanders and Australians taken prisoner exceeds 9,000 officers and men.

The German share of the booty alone, according to the estimates at present available, amounts to more than half a million rifles, far more than 1,000 guns, many thousand machine-guns and anti-aircraft machine-guns, vehicles, and large amounts of ammunition . . . .

The losses of the German Army and the German Air Force as well as those of the SS troops in this campaign are the smallest that we have ever suffered so far. The German armed forces have in fighting against Yugoslavia and Greece as well as against the British in Greece lost:

Army and SS Troops - Fifty-seven officers and 1,042 noncommissioned officers and men killed, 181 officers and 3,571 noncommissioned officers and men wounded, and 13 officers and 372 noncommissioned officers and men missing.

Air Force - Ten officers and 42 noncommissioned officers and men killed and 36 officers and 104 noncommissioned officers and men missing.

Once more I can only repeat that we feel the hardship of the sacrifice borne by the families concerned. The entire German nation expresses to them its heartfelt gratitude.

Taking the measures as a whole, however, the losses suffered are so small that they constitute supreme justification, first, for the planning and timing of this campaign; second for the conduct of operations; third, for the manner in which they were carried through.

The training of our officers is excellent beyond comparison The high standard of efficiency of our soldiers, the superiority of our equipment, the quality of our munitions and the indomitable courage of all ranks have combined to lead at such small sacrifice to a success of truly decisive historical importance.

Churchill, one of the most hopeless dabblers in.strategy, thus managed to lose two theaters of war at one single blow. The fact that this man, who in any other country would be court-martialed, gained fresh admiration as Prime Minister cannot be construed as an expression of magnanimity such as was accorded by Roman senators to generals honorably defeated in battle. It is merely proof of that perpetual blindness with which the gods afflict those whom they are about to destroy.

The consequences of this campaign are extraordinary. In view of the fact that a small set of conspirators in Belgrade again were able to foment trouble in the service of extracontinental interests, the radical elimination of this danger means the removal of an element of tension for the whole of Europe.

The Danube as an important waterway is thus safeguarded against any further act of sabotage. Traffic has been resumed in full.

Apart from the modest correction of its frontiers, which were infringed as a result of the outcome of the World War, the Reich has no special territorial interests in these parts. As far as politics are concerned we are merely interested in safeguarding peace in this region, while in the realm of economics we wish to see an order that will allow the production of goods to be developed and the exchange of products to be resumed in the interests of all.

It is, however, only in accordance with supreme justice if those interests are also taken into account that are founded upon ethnographical, historical, or economic conditions.

I can assure you that I look into the future with perfect tranquillity and great confidence. The German Reich and its allies represent power, military, economic and, above all, in moral respects, which is superior to any possible coalition in the world. The German armed forces will always do their part whenever it may be necessary. The confidence of the German people will always accompany their soldiers.

LA PASSIONARIA

Powerful speakers opposed Hitler, such as Churchill, and Roosevelt, among the best was a woman Dolores Ibarurri "La Passionaria" {1938} a Spanish Communist leader whose speeches inspired the resistance to the Falange, and to the Nazi war machine at work in Spain.

Dolores Ibárruri, La Pasionaria Barcelona, November 1, 1938, giving her farewell address to The International Brigades: Notice she starts with a bang, the first sentence was delivered very dramatically.

The Spanish people would rather die on its feet than live on its knees. And do not forget, and let no one forget, that if today it is our turn to resist fascist aggression, the struggle will not end in Spain. Today it's us; but if the Spanish people is allowed to be crushed, you will be next, all of Europe will have to face aggression and war.

It is very difficult to say a few words in farewell to the heroes of the International Brigades, because of what they are and what they represent. A feeling of sorrow, an infinite grief catches our throat - sorrow for those who are going away, for the soldiers of the highest ideal of human redemption, exiles from their countries, persecuted by the tyrants of all peoples - grief for those who will stay here forever mingled with the Spanish soil, in the very depth of our heart, hallowed by our feeling of eternal gratitude.

From all peoples, from all races, you came to us like brothers, like sons of immortal Spain; and in the hardest days of the war, when the capital of the Spanish Republic was threatened, it was you, gallant comrades of the International Brigades, who helped save the city with your fighting enthusiasm, your heroism and your spirit of sacrifice. - And Jarama and Guadalajara, Brunete and Belchite, Levante and the Ebro, in immortal verses sing of the courage, the sacrifice, the daring, th discipline of the men of the International Brigades.

For the first time in the history of the peoples' struggles, there was the spectacle, breathtaking in its grandeur, of the formation of International Brigades to help save a threatened country's freedom and independence - the freedom and independence of our Spanish land. Communists, Socialists, Anarchists, Republicans - men of different colors, differing ideology, antagonistic religions --- yet all profoundly loving liberty and justice, they came and offered themselves to us unconditionally. They gave us everything --- their youth or their maturity; their science or their experience; their blood and their lives; their hopes and aspirations --- and they asked us for nothing. But yes, it must be said, they did want a post in battle, they aspired to the honor of dying for us.
Banners of Spain! Salute these many heroes! Be lowered to honor so many martyrs! Mothers! Women! When the years pass by and the wounds of war are stanched; when the memory of the sad and bloody days dissipates in a present of liberty, of peace and of wellbeing; when the rancors have died out and pride in a free country is felt equally by all Spaniards, speak to your children. Tell them of these men of the International Brigades.Recount for them how, coming over seas and mountains, crossing frontiers bristling with bayonets, sought by raving dogs thirsting to tear their flesh, these men reached our country as crusaders for freedom, to fight and die for Spain's liberty and independence threatened by German and Italian fascism. They gave up everything --- their loves, their countries, home and fortune, fathers, mothers, wives, brothers, sisters and children --- and they came and said to us: ``We are here. Your cause, Spain's cause, is ours. It is the cause of all advanced and progressive mankind."

Today many are departing. Thousands remain, shrouded in Spanish earth, profoundly remembered by all Spaniards. Comrades of the International Brigades: Political reasons, reasons of state, the welfare of that very cause for which you offered your blood with boundless generosity, are sending you back, some to your own countries and others to forced exile. You can go proudly. You are history. You are legend. You are the heroic example of democracy's solidarity and universality in the face of the vile and accommodating spirit of those who interpret democratic principles with their eyes on hoards of wealth or corporate shares which they want to safeguard from all risk.

We shall not forget you; and, when the olive tree of peace is in flower, entwined with the victory laurels of the Republic of Spain --- return!
Return to our side for here you will find a homeland --- those who have no country or friends, who must live deprived of friendship --- all, all will have the affection and gratitude of the Spanish people who today and tomorrow will shout with enthusiasm ---

Long live the heroes of the International Brigades!

President John F. Kennedy

The backdrop to this speech was that George C. Wallace had just made his place in history as an arch segregationist by standing in the school house door to personally block the entry of black students.

President Kennedy on racism:

Good evening, my fellow citizens:

This afternoon, following a series of threats and defiant statements, the presence of Alabama National Guardsmen was required on the University of Alabama to carry out the final and unequivocal order of the United States District Court of the Northern District of Alabama. That order called for the admission of two clearly qualified young Alabama residents who happened to have been born Negro. That they were admitted peacefully on the campus is due in good measure to the conduct of the students of the University of Alabama, who met their responsibilities in a constructive way.

I hope that every American, regardless of where he lives, will stop and examine his conscience about this and other related incidents. This Nation was founded by men of many nations and backgrounds. It was founded on the principle that all men are created equal, and that the rights of every man are diminished when the rights of one man are threatened.

Today, we are committed to a worldwide struggle to promote and protect the rights of all who wish to be free. And when Americans are sent to Vietnam or West Berlin, we do not ask for whites only. It ought to be possible, therefore, for American students of any color to attend any public institution they select without having to be backed up by troops. It ought to be possible for American consumers of any color to receive equal service in places of public accommodation, such as hotels and restaurants and theaters and retail stores, without being forced to resort to demonstrations in the street, and it ought to be possible for American citizens of any color to register and to vote in a free election without interference or fear of reprisal. It ought to be possible, in short, for every American to enjoy the privileges of

100

being American without regard to his race or his color. In short, every American ought to have the right to be treated as he would wish to be treated, as one would wish his children to be treated. But this is not the case.

The Negro baby born in America today, regardless of the section of the State in which he is born, has about one-half as much chance of completing a high school as a white baby born in the same place on the same day, one-third as much chance of completing college, one-third as much chance of becoming a professional man, twice as much chance of becoming unemployed, about one-seventh as much chance of earning $10,000 a year, a life expectancy which is 7 years shorter, and the prospects of earning only half as much.

This is not a sectional issue. Difficulties over segregation and discrimination exist in every city, in every State of the Union, producing in many cities a rising tide of discontent that threatens the public safety. Nor is this a partisan issue. In a time of domestic crisis men of good will and generosity should be able to unite regardless of party or politics. This is not even a legal or legislative issue alone. It is better to settle these matters in the courts than on the streets, and new laws are needed at every level, but law alone cannot make men see right. We are confronted primarily with a moral issue. It is as old as the Scriptures and is as clear as the American Constitution.

The heart of the question is whether all Americans are to be afforded equal rights and equal opportunities, whether we are going to treat our fellow Americans as we want to be treated. If an American, because his skin is dark, cannot eat lunch in a restaurant open to the public, if he cannot send his children to the best public school available, if he cannot vote for the public officials who will represent him, if, in short, he cannot enjoy the full and free life which all of us want, then who among us would be content to have the color of his skin changed and stand in his place? Who among us would then be content with the counsels of patience and delay?

One hundred years of delay have passed since President Lincoln freed the slaves, yet their heirs, their grandsons, are not fully free. They are not yet freed from the bonds of injustice. They are not yet freed from social and economic oppression. And this Nation, for all its hopes and all its boasts, will not be fully free until all its citizens are free.

We preach freedom around the world, and we mean it, and we cherish our freedom here at home, but are we to say to the world, and much more importantly, to each other that this is the land of the free except for the Negroes; that we have no second-class citizens except Negroes; that we have no class or caste system, no ghettoes, no master race except with respect to Negroes?

Now the time has come for this Nation to fulfill its promise. The events in Birmingham and elsewhere have so increased the cries for equality that no city or State or legislative body can prudently choose to ignore them. The fires of frustration and discord are burning in every city, North and South, where legal remedies are not at hand. Redress is sought in the streets, in demonstrations, parades, and protests which create tensions and threaten violence and threaten lives.

We face, therefore, a moral crisis as a country and a people. It cannot be met by repressive police action. It cannot be left to increased demonstrations in the streets. It cannot be quieted by token moves or talk. It is a time to act in the Congress, in your State and local legislative body and, above all, in all of our daily lives. It is not enough to pin the blame on others, to say this a problem of one section of the country or another, or deplore the facts that we face. A great change is at hand, and our task, our obligation, is to make that revolution, that change, peaceful and constructive for all. Those who do nothing are inviting shame, as well as violence. Those who act boldly are recognizing right, as well as reality.

Next week I shall ask the Congress of the United States to act, to make a commitment it has not fully made in this century to the proposition that race has no place in American life or law. The Federal judiciary has upheld that proposition in a series of forthright cases. The Executive Branch has adopted that proposition in the conduct of its affairs, including the employment of Federal personnel, the use of Federal facilities, and the sale of federally financed housing. But there are other necessary measures which only the Congress can provide, and they must be provided at this session. The old code of equity law under which we live commands for every wrong a remedy, but in too many communities, in too many parts of the country, wrongs are inflicted on Negro citizens and there are no remedies at law. Unless the Congress acts, their only remedy is the street.

I am, therefore, asking the Congress to enact legislation giving all Americans the right to be served in facilities which are open to the public -- hotels, restaurants, theaters, retail stores, and similar establishments. This seems to me to be an elementary right. Its denial is an arbitrary indignity that no American in 1963 should have to endure, but many do.

I have recently met with scores of business leaders urging them to take voluntary action to end this discrimination, and I have been encouraged by their response, and in the last two weeks over 75 cities have seen progress made in desegregating these kinds of facilities. But many are unwilling to act alone, and for this reason, nationwide legislation is needed if we are to move this problem from the streets to the courts.

I'm also asking the Congress to authorize the Federal Government to participate more fully in lawsuits designed to end segregation in public education. We have succeeded in persuading many districts to desegregate voluntarily. Dozens have admitted Negroes without violence. Today, a Negro is attending a State-supported institution in every one of our 50 States, but the pace is very slow.

Too many Negro children entering segregated grade schools at the time of the Supreme Court's decision nine years ago will enter segregated high schools this fall, having suffered a loss which can never be restored. The lack of an adequate education denies the Negro a chance to get a decent job.

The orderly implementation of the Supreme Court decision, therefore, cannot be left solely to those who may not have the economic resources to carry the legal action or who may be subject to harassment.

Other features will be also requested, including greater protection for the right to vote. But legislation, I repeat, cannot solve this problem alone. It must be solved in the homes of every American in every community across our country. In this respect I want to pay tribute to those citizens North and South who've been working in their communities to make life better for all. They are acting not out of sense of legal duty but out of a sense of human decency. Like our soldiers and sailors in all parts of the world they are meeting freedom's challenge on the firing line, and I salute them for their honor and their courage.

My fellow Americans, this is a problem which faces us all -- in every city of the North as well as the South. Today, there are Negroes unemployed, two or three times as many compared to whites, inadequate education, moving into the large cities, unable to find work, young people particularly out of work without hope, denied equal rights, denied the opportunity to eat at a restaurant or a lunch counter or go to a movie theater, denied the right to a decent education, denied almost today the right to attend a State university even though qualified. It seems to me that these are matters which concern us all, not merely Presidents or Congressmen or Governors, but every citizen of the United States.

This is one country. It has become one country because all of us and all the people who came here had an equal chance to develop their talents. We cannot say to ten percent of the population that you can't have that right; that your children cannot have the chance to develop whatever talents they have; that the only way that they are going to get their rights is to go in the street and demonstrate. I think we owe them and we owe ourselves a better country than that.

Therefore, I'm asking for your help in making it easier for us to move ahead and to provide the kind of equality of treatment which we would want ourselves; to give a chance for every child to be educated to the limit of his talents.

As I've said before, not every child has an equal talent or an equal ability or equal motivation, but they should have the equal right to develop their talent and their ability and their motivation, to make something of themselves.

We have a right to expect that the Negro community will be responsible, will uphold the law, but they have a right to expect that the law will be fair, that the Constitution will be color blind, as Justice Harlan said at the turn of the century.

This is what we're talking about and this is a matter which concerns this country and what it stands for, and in meeting it I ask the support of all our citizens.

Thank you very much.

BARBARA JORDAN

The background for this speech is that it was delivered at the height of the Watergate crises and led to the collapse of political support for President Nixon. She had a voice that sounded as if Moses were a woman that is how he would sound.

Barbara Jordan - Statement on House Judiciary Proceedings to Impeach President Richard Nixon delivered 25 July 1974, House Judiciary Committee

Barbara Jordan: Statement on the Articles of Impeachment

Mr. Chairman, I join my colleague Mr. Rangel in thanking you for giving the junior members of this committee the glorious opportunity of sharing the pain of this inquiry. Mr. Chairman, you are a strong man, and it has not been easy but we have tried as best we can to give you as much assistance as possible.

Earlier today, we heard the beginning of the Preamble to the Constitution of the United States, "We, the people". It's a very eloquent beginning. But when that document was completed, on the seventeenth of September in 1787, I was not included in that "We, the people". I felt somehow for many years that George Washington and Alexander Hamilton just left me out by mistake. But through the process of amendment, interpretation, and court decision, I have finally been included in "We, the people". Today I am an inquisitor. An hyperbole would not be fictional and would not overstate the solemnness that I feel right now. My faith in the Constitution is whole; it is complete; it is total. And I am not going to sit here and be an idle spectator to the diminution, the subversion, the destruction, of the Constitution.

106

"Who can so properly be the inquisitors for the nation as the representatives of the nation themselves?" (Federalist, no. 65). The subject of its jurisdiction are those offenses which proceed from the misconduct of public men." That is what we are talking about. In other words, the jurisdiction comes from the abuse of violation of some public trust. It is wrong, I suggest, it is a misreading of the Constitution for any member here to assert that for a member to vote for an article of impeachment means that that member must be convinced that the president should be removed from office. The Constitution doesn't say that. The powers relating to impeachment are an essential check in the hands of the body of the legislature against and upon the encroachments of the executive. The division between the two branches of the legislature, the House and the Senate, assigning to the one the right to accuse and to the other the right to judge, the framers of this Constitution were very astute. They did not make the accusers and the judges the same person.

We know the nature of impeachment. We have been talking about it awhile now. "It is chiefly designed for the president and his high ministers" to somehow be called into account. It is designed to "bridle" the executive if he engages in excesses. "It is designed as a method of national inquest into the public men." The framers confined in the congress the power if need be, to remove the president in order to strike a delicate balance between a president swollen with power and grown tyrannical, and preservation of the independence of the executive. The nature of impeachment is a narrowly channeled exception to the separation-of-powers maxim; the federal convention of 1787 said that. The framers limited impeachment to high crimes and misdemeanors and discounted and opposed the term "maladministration." "It is to be used only for great misdemeanors," so it was said in the North Carolina ratification convention. And in the Virginia ratification convention: "We do not trust our liberty to a particular branch. We need one branch to check the others."The North Carolina ratification convention: "No one need be afraid that officers who commit oppression will pass

107

with immunity." "Prosecutions of impeachments will seldom fail to agitate the passions of the whole community," said Hamilton in the Federalist Papers, no. 65. "And to divide it into parties more or less friendly or inimical to the accused." I do not mean political parties in that sense. The drawing of political lines goes to the motivation behind impeachment; but impeachment must proceed within the confines of the constitutional term "high crimes and misdemeanors." Of the impeachment process, it was Woodrow Wilson who said that "nothing short of the grossest offenses against the plain law of the land will suffice to give them speed and effectiveness. Indignation so great as to overgrow party interest may secure a conviction; but nothing else can." Common sense would be revolted if we engaged upon this process for petty reasons. Congress has a lot to do: Appropriation, Tax Reform, Health Insurance, Campaign Finance Reform, Housing, Environmental Protection, Energy Sufficiency, Mass Transportation.

Pettiness cannot be allowed to stand in the face of such overwhelming problems. So today we are not being petty. We are trying to be big because the task we have before us is a big one. This morning, in a discussion of the evidence, we were told that the evidence which purports to support the allegations of misuse of the CIA by the President is thin. We are told that that evidence is insufficient.

What that recital of the evidence this morning did not include is what the President did know on June the 23rd, 1972. The President did know that it was Republican money, that it was money from the Committee for the Re-Election of the President, which was found in the possession of one of the burglars arrested on June the 17th. What the President did know on the 23rd of June was the prior activities of E. Howard Hunt, which included his participation in the break-in of Daniel Ellsberg's psychiatrist, which included Howard Hunt's participation in the Dita Beard ITT affair, which included Howard Hunt's fabrication of cables designed to discredit the Kennedy administration.

We were further cautioned today that perhaps these proceedings ought to be delayed because certainly there would be new evidence forthcoming from the president of the United States. There has not even been an obfuscated indication that this committee would receive any additional materials from the President. The committee subpoena is outstanding, and if the president wants to supply that material, the committee sits here. The fact is that on yesterday, the American people waited with great anxiety for eight hours, not knowing whether their president would obey an order of the Supreme Court of the United States.

At this point, I would like to juxtapose a few of the impeachment criteria with some of actions the President has engaged in. Impeachment criteria: James Madison, from the Virginia ratification convention. "If the president be connected in any suspicious manner with any person and there be grounds to believe that he will shelter him, he may be impeached." We have heard time and time again that the evidence reflects the payment to defendants of money. The president had knowledge that these funds were being paid and these were funds collected for the 1972 presidential campaign. We know that the president met with Mr. Henry Petersen twenty-seven times to discuss matters related to Watergate and immediately thereafter met with the very persons who were implicated in the information Mr. Petersen was receiving and transmitting to the president. The words are "if the president be connected in any suspicious manner with any person and there be grounds to believe that he will shelter that person, he may be impeached."Justice Story: "Impeachment is intended for occasional and extraordinary cases where a superior power acting for the whole people is put into operation to protect their rights and rescue their liberties from violations."

We know about the Huston plan. We know about the break-in of the psychiatrist's office. We know that there was absolute complete direction in August 1971 when the

109

president instructed Ehrlichman to "do whatever is necessary." This instruction led to a surreptitious entry into Dr. Fielding's office. "Protect their rights." "Rescue their liberties from violation." The South Carolina ratification convention impeachment criteria: those are impeachable "who behave amiss or betray their public trust."

Beginning shortly after the Watergate break-in and continuing to the present time, the president has engaged in a series of public statements and actions designed to thwart the lawful investigation by government prosecutors. Moreover, the president has made public announcements and assertions bearing on the Watergate case which the evidence will show he knew to be false. These assertions, false assertions, impeachable, those who misbehave. Those who "behave amiss or betray their public trust." James Madison again at the Constitutional Convention: "A president is impeachable if he attempts to subvert the Constitution." The Constitution charges the president with the task of taking care that the laws be faithfully executed, and yet the president has counseled his aides to commit perjury, willfully disregarded the secrecy of grand jury proceedings, concealed surreptitious entry, attempted to compromise a federal judge while publicly displaying his cooperation with the processes of criminal justice."A president is impeachable if he attempts to subvert the Constitution."If the impeachment provision in the Constitution of the United States will not reach the offenses charged here, then perhaps that 18th century Constitution should be abandoned to a 20th century paper shredder. Has the president committed offenses, and planned, and directed, and acquiesced in a course of conduct which the Constitution will not tolerate? That's the question. We know that. We know the question. We should now forthwith proceed to answer the question. It is reason, and not passion, which must guide our deliberations, guide our debate, and guide our decision.

Senator John F. Kennedy

Candidate John Kennedy during his 1960 election campaign delivered this speech on anti-Catholic bias, it virtually eliminated the issue in American public life. As a historian, despite JFKs faults, I always admired the fact that even though he volunteered for combat in WWII even though with his millions he could have hid out in Mexico, as others such as John Wayne did. The speech was very effective, after the speech, the candidates religion ceased to be an issue, for after all as the President pointed out, there are no religious tests on battlefields.

Reverend Meza, Reverend Reck, I'm grateful for your generous invitation to state my views.

While the so-called religious issue is necessarily and properly the chief topic here tonight, I want to emphasize from the outset that I believe that we have far more critical issues in the 1960 campaign; the spread of Communist influence, until it now festers only 90 miles from the coast of Florida -- the humiliating treatment of our President and Vice President by those who no longer respect our power -- the hungry children I saw in West Virginia, the old people who cannot pay their doctors bills, the families forced to give up their farms -- an America with too many slums, with too few schools, and too late to the moon and outer space. These are the real issues which should decide this campaign. And they are not religious issues -- for war and hunger and ignorance and despair know no religious barrier.

But because I am a Catholic, and no Catholic has ever been elected President, the real issues in this campaign have been obscured -- perhaps deliberately, in some quarters less responsible than this. So it is apparently necessary for me to state once again -- not what kind of church I believe in, for that should be important only to me -- but what kind of America I believe in.

I believe in an America where the separation of church and state is absolute; where no Catholic prelate would tell the President -- should he be Catholic -- how to act, and no Protestant minister would tell his parishioners for whom to vote; where no church or church school is granted any public funds or political preference, and where no man is denied public office merely because his religion differs from the President who might appoint him, or the people who might elect him.

I believe in an America that is officially neither Catholic, Protestant nor Jewish; where no public official either requests or accept instructions on public policy from the Pope, the National Council of Churches or any other ecclesiastical source; where no religious body seeks to impose its will directly or indirectly upon the general populace or the public acts of its officials, and where religious liberty is so indivisible that an act against one church is treated as an act against all.

For while this year it may be a Catholic against whom the finger of suspicion is pointed, in other years it has been -- and may someday be again -- a Jew, or a Quaker, or a Unitarian, or a Baptist. It was Virginia's harassment of Baptist preachers, for example, that led to Jefferson's statute of religious freedom. Today, I may be the victim, but tomorrow it may be you -- until the whole fabric of our harmonious society is ripped apart at a time of great national peril.

Finally, I believe in an America where religious intolerance will someday end -- where all men and all churches are treated as equals, where every man has the same right to attend or not to attend the church of his choice, where there is no Catholic vote, no anti-Catholic vote, no bloc voting of any kind, and where Catholics, Protestants, and Jews, at both the lay and the pastoral levels, will refrain from those attitudes of disdain and division which have so often marred their works in the past, and promote instead the American ideal of brotherhood.

That is the kind of America in which I believe. And it represents the kind of Presidency in which I believe, a great office that must be neither humbled by making it the instrument of any religious group

112

nor tarnished by arbitrarily withholding its occupancy from the members of any one religious group. I believe in a President whose views on religion are his own private affair, neither imposed upon him by the nation, nor imposed by the nation upon him as a condition to holding that office.

I would not look with favor upon a President working to subvert the first amendment's guarantees of religious liberty. Nor would our system of checks and balances permit him to do so. And neither do I look with favor upon those who would work to subvert Article VI of the Constitution by requiring a religious test, even by indirection. For if they disagree with that safeguard, they should be out openly working to repeal it.

I want a Chief Executive whose public acts are responsible to all and obligated to none, who can attend any ceremony, service, or dinner his office may appropriately require of him to fulfill; and whose fulfillment of his Presidential office is not limited or conditioned by any religious oath, ritual, or obligation.

This is the kind of America I believe in -- and this is the kind of America I fought for in the South Pacific, and the kind my brother died for in Europe. No one suggested then that we might have a divided loyalty, that we did not believe in liberty, or that we belonged to a disloyal group that threatened "the freedoms for which our forefathers died."

And in fact this is the kind of America for which our forefathers did when they fled here to escape religious test oaths that denied office to members of less favored churches -- when they fought for the Constitution, the Bill of Rights, the Virginia Statute of Religious Freedom -- and when they fought at the shrine I visited today, the Alamo. For side by side with Bowie and Crockett died Fuentes, and McCafferty, and Bailey, and Badillo, and Carey -- but no one knows whether they were Catholics or not. For there was no religious test there.

I ask you tonight to follow in that tradition -- to judge me on the basis of 14 years in the Congress, on my declared stands against an

Ambassador to the Vatican, against unconstitutional aid to parochial schools, and against any boycott of the public schools -- which I attended myself. And instead of doing this, do not judge me on the basis of these pamphlets and publications we all have seen that carefully select quotations out of context from the statements of Catholic church leaders, usually in other countries, frequently in other centuries, and rarely relevant to any situation here. And always omitting, of course, the statement of the American Bishops in 1948 which strongly endorsed Church-State separation, and which more nearly reflects the views of almost every American Catholic.

I do not consider these other quotations binding upon my public acts. Why should you?

But let me say, with respect to other countries, that I am wholly opposed to the State being used by any religious group, Catholic or Protestant, to compel, prohibit, or prosecute the free exercise of any other religion. And that goes for any persecution, at any time, by anyone, in any country. And I hope that you and I condemn with equal fervor those nations which deny their Presidency to Protestants, and those which deny it to Catholics. And rather than cite the misdeeds of those who differ, I would also cite the record of the Catholic Church in such nations as France and Ireland, and the independence of such statesmen as De Gaulle and Adenauer.

But let me stress again that these are my views.

For contrary to common newspaper usage, I am not the Catholic candidate for President.

I am the Democratic Party's candidate for President who happens also to be a Catholic.

I do not speak for my church on public matters; and the church does not speak for me. Whatever issue may come before me as President, if I should be elected, on birth control, divorce, censorship, gambling or any other subject, I will make my decision in accordance with these views -- in accordance with what my conscience tells me to be in the national interest, and without regard to outside religious pressure or dictates. And no power or threat of punishment could cause me to decide otherwise.

But if the time should ever come -- and I do not concede any conflict to be remotely possible -- when my office would require me to either violate my conscience or violate the national interest, then I would resign the office; and I hope any conscientious public servant would do likewise.

But I do not intend to apologize for these views to my critics of either Catholic or Protestant faith; nor do I intend to disavow either my views or my church in order to win this election.

If I should lose on the real issues, I shall return to my seat in the Senate, satisfied that I'd tried my best and was fairly judged.

But if this election is decided on the basis that 40 million Americans lost their chance of being President on the day they were baptized, then it is the whole nation that will be the loser, in the eyes of Catholics and non-Catholics around the world, in the eyes of history, and in the eyes of our own people.

But if, on the other hand, I should win this election, then I shall devote every effort of mind and spirit to fulfilling the oath of the Presidency -- practically identical, I might add, with the oath I have taken for 14 years in the Congress. For without reservation, I can, "solemnly swear that I will faithfully execute the office of President of the United States, and will to the best of my ability preserve, protect, and defend the Constitution -- so help me God.

www.ingramcontent.com/pod-product-compliance
Lightning Source LLC
Chambersburg PA
CBHW071207280526
45787CB00002B/593